Y0-CUQ-232

Sacred Music

Part 2

Recent Researches in Music

A-R Editions publishes seven series of critical editions, spanning the history of Western music, American music, and oral traditions.

Recent Researches in the Music of the Middle Ages and Early Renaissance
Charles M. Atkinson, general editor

Recent Researches in the Music of the Renaissance
James Haar, general editor

Recent Researches in the Music of the Baroque Era
Christoph Wolff, general editor

Recent Researches in the Music of the Classical Era
Neal Zaslaw, general editor

Recent Researches in the Music of the Nineteenth and Early Twentieth Centuries
Rufus Hallmark, general editor

Recent Researches in American Music
John M. Graziano, general editor

Recent Researches in the Oral Traditions of Music
Philip V. Bohlman, general editor

Each edition in *Recent Researches* is devoted to works by a single composer or to a single genre. The content is chosen for its high quality and historical importance and is edited according to the scholarly standards that govern the making of all reliable editions.

For information on establishing a standing order to any of our series, or for editorial guidelines on submitting proposals, please contact:

A-R Editions, Inc.
Middleton, Wisconsin

800 736-0070 (North American book orders)
608 836-9000 (phone)
608 831-8200 (fax)
http://www.areditions.com

Recent Researches in the Music of the Baroque Era, 165

Antoine Boesset

Sacred Music

Part 2
Canticles, Psalms, and Masses

Edited by Peter Bennett

A-R Editions, Inc., Middleton, Wisconsin

Printed in the United States of America

ISBN-13: 978-0-89579-685-1
ISBN-10: 0-89579-685-6
ISSN: 0484-0828

♾ The paper used in this publication meets the minimum requirements of the American National Standard for Information Sciences—Permanence of Paper for Printed Library Materials, ANSI Z39.48-1992.

Contents

Acknowledgments

Work on this edition was greatly assisted by a number of individuals and organizations. I am grateful to Catherine Massip and the staff at the Music Department of the Bibliothèque nationale de France for their assistance and courtesy and for permission to publish photographic reproductions. I am also indebted to my godparents, Jean and Bernard Lefèvre, whose hospitality in Paris enabled me to carry out the research that led to this edition. A W. P. Jones Faculty Development grant from Case Western Reserve University enabled me to complete my work in a timely manner, as did the assistance of Nathaniel Wood, who helped with preliminary stages of the edition. Finally, I am grateful to Jean Duron and Thomas Lecomte of the Centre de Musique Baroque à Versailles for their stimulating comments about Boesset and sacred music, and for the support of numerous other colleagues who share my interest in bringing the music of Louis XIII to a wider audience.

Plates

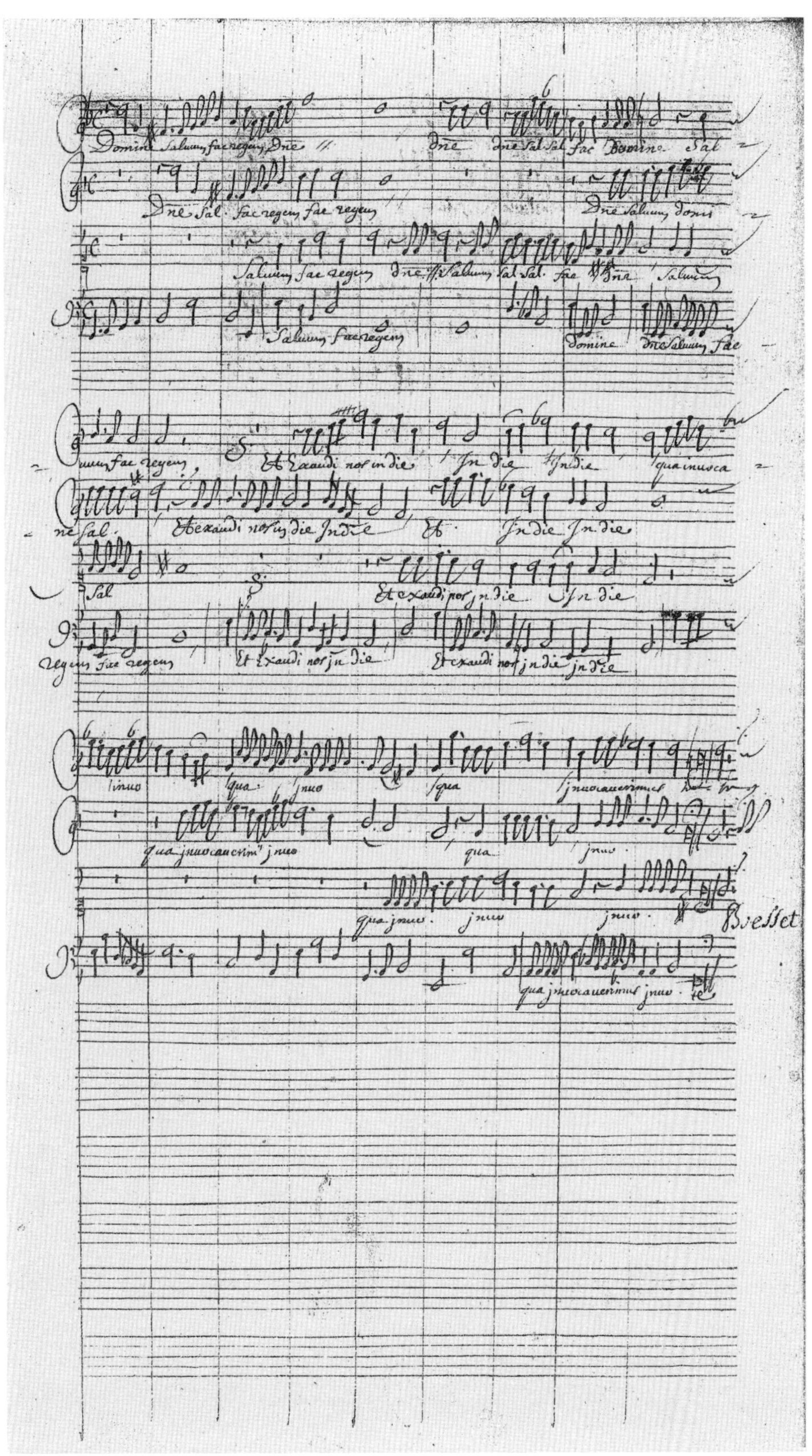

Plate 1. Antoine Boesset, "Domine salvum fac regem (2)" with attribution to "Boesset." Paris, Bibliothèque nationale de France, Département de la Musique, Rés. V^{ma} ms. 571, folio 1v. Reproduced with permission from the Bibliothèque nationale de France.

Plate 2. Antoine Boesset, Magnificat (1), measures 1–11, with bass line sketches and psalm tone concordant with the *Antiphonier . . . de Montmartre*. Paris, Bibliothèque nationale de France, Département de la Musique, Rés. V^{ma} ms. 571, folio 155v. Reproduced with permission from the Bibliothèque nationale de France.

520 Chant des Pſalmes.

cem o ra ti o nis meæ.

Pſal. DE profundis cla ma ui ad te Domine :

Domine exaudi vocem meam.

MAgni ficat, a ni ma mea Dominum.

Et exul ta uit ſpiritus me us, in Deo ſa-

lu ta ri me o.

MAgni ficat, a nima me a Dominum.

Et ex ul ta uit ſpiri tus me us, in De o

ſalutari

Plate 3. *Antiphonier Bénédictin pour les réligieuses du Royal et célèbre monastère de Montmartre* (Paris: L. Sevestre, 1646), page 520, showing Magnificat tones concordant with Rés. 571. Paris, Bibliothèque nationale de France. Reproduced with permission from the Bibliothèque nationale de France.

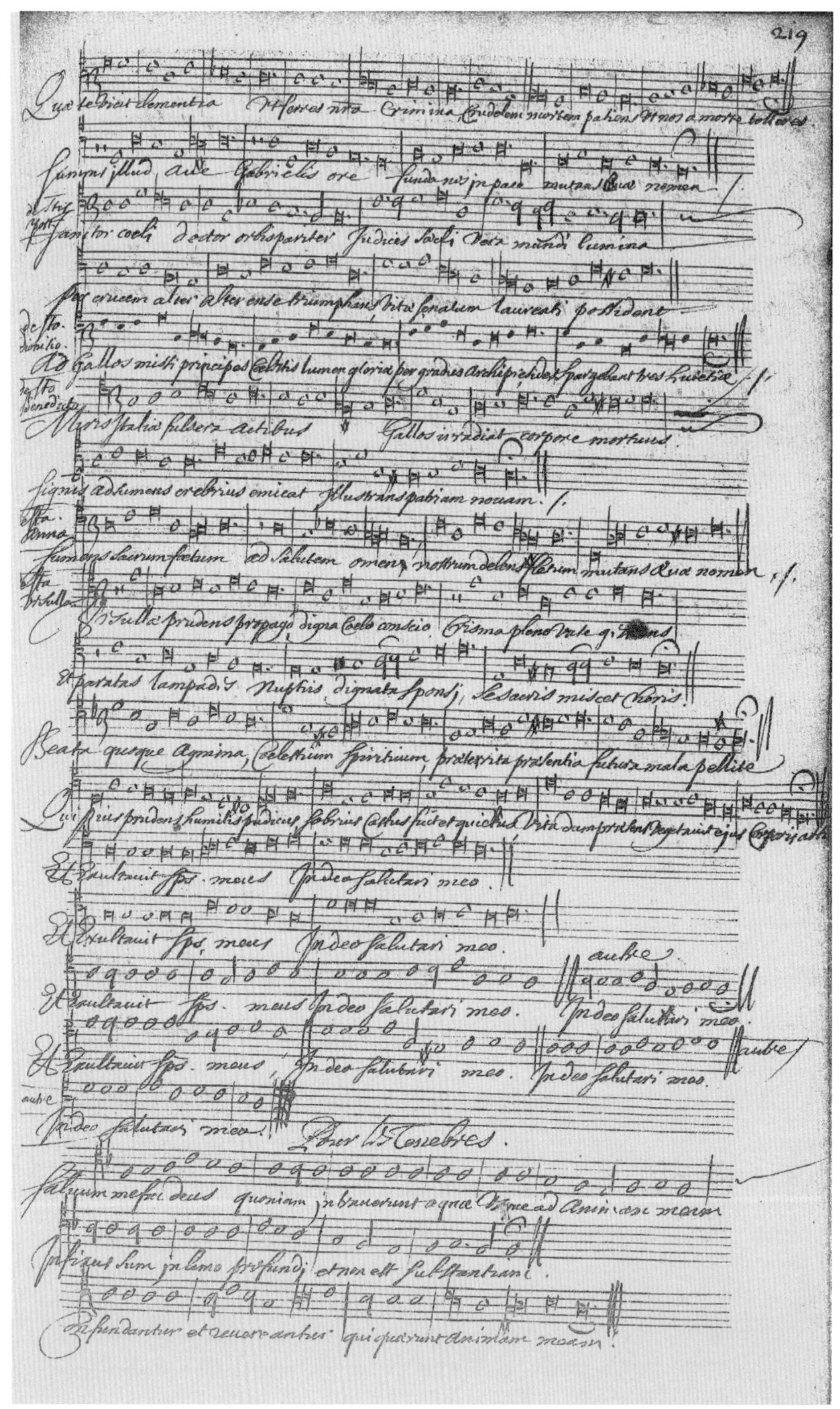

Plate 4. Rhythmicized versions of hymn melodies, Magnificat tones, and Tenebrae tones. Paris, Bibliothèque nationale de France, Département de la Musique, Rés. V^{ma} ms. 571, folio 219r. Reproduced with permission from the Bibliothèque nationale de France.

Canticles

1. Magnificat (1)

9

[D1] Qui- a re- spe- xit hu- mi- li- ta- tem an- cil- lae su-

[B.c.]

14

[D1] -ae: om- nes

[D2] ec- ce e- nim ex hoc be- a- tam me di- cent

[D3] ec- ce e- nim ex hoc be- a- tam me di- cent

[HC] ec- ce e- nim ex hoc be- a- tam me di- cent

[B] ec- ce e- nim ex hoc be- a- tam me di- cent

[B.c.]

19

ge- ne- ra- - ti- o- nes.

om- nes ge- ne- ra- ti- o- nes.

om- nes ge- ne- ra- ti- o- nes.

om- nes ge- ne- ra- ti- o nes.

om- nes ge- ne- ra- ti- o- nes.

25
Plain chant
Qui- a fe- cit mi- hi ma- gna qui po- tens est: et san- ctum no- men e- jus.
26
[D1]
Et mi- se- ri- cor- di-
[D2]
[D3]
[HC]
[B]
[B.c.]
28
-a e- jus a pro- ge- ni- e in pro- ge- ni- es ti- men-
a pro- ge- ni- e in pro- ge- ni- es
a pro- ge- ni- e in pro- ge- ni- es
a pro- ge- ni- e in pro- ge- ni- es
a pro- ge- ni- e in pro- ge- ni- es

33
- ti- bus e- um, ti- men- ti- bus e- um, ti- men- ti-
ti- men- ti- bus, ti- men- ti- bus e- um,
ti- men- - ti- bus e- um, ti-
ti- men- - ti- bus e- um,
ti- men- - ti- bus e- um, ti-
38
-bus, ti- men- ti- bus e- um.
ti- men- ti- bus e- um.
-men- ti- bus e- um.
ti- men- ti- bus e- um.
-men- ti- bus e- um.
41
Plain chant
Fe- cit po- ten- ti- am in bra- chi- o su- o:

(41)
di- sper- sit su- per- bos men- te cor- dis su- i.
42
[D1]
De- po- su- it po-ten- tes de se- de,
[D2]
De- po- su- it po- ten- - tes de
[D3]
[HC]
[B]
[B.c.]
45
de se- de, et ex- al- ta- vit hu- mi- les, et ex- al- ta- vit hu- mi- les, et ex- al-
se- de, et ex- al- ta- vit hu- mi- les, et ex- al-
et ex- al- ta- vit hu- mi- les, et ex- al-
et ex- al- ta- vit hu- mi- les, et ex- al-
et ex- al- ta- vit hu- mi- les, et ex- al-

51
-ta- vit hu- mi- les.
-ta- vit hu- mi- les.
-ta- vit hu- mi- les.
-ta- vit hu- mi- les.
-ta- vit hu- mi- les.
53
Plain chant
E- su- ri- en- tes im- ple- vit bo- nis: et di- vi- tes di- mi- sit i- na- nes.
54
[D1]
[D2]
Su- sce- - pit Is- ra- el pu-
[D3]
Su- sce- pit, su- sce- pit Is- ra- el pu-
[HC]
Su- sce- pit Is- ra- el, su- sce- pit Is- ra- el pu-
[B]
Su- sce- pit Is- ra- el pu- e- rum, pu-
[B.c.]

59
re- cor- da- tus mi- se- ri- cor- di- ae, mi- se- ri-
-e- rum su- um,
-e- rum su- um, re- cor- da- tus mi- se- ri- cor- di- ae, mi- se- ri-
-e- rum su- um, re- cor- da- tus mi-
-e- rum su- um, re- cor- da- tus mi- se- ri- cor-
64
-cor- di- ae su- ae, mi- se- ri- cor- di- ae su- ae.
mi- se- ri- cor- di- ae su- ae.
-cor- di- ae su- ae, mi- se- ri- cor- di- ae su- ae.
-se- ri- cor- di- ae su- ae, mi- se- ri- cor- di- ae su- ae.
- di- ae su- ae, mi- se- ri- cor- di- ae su- ae.

70
[D1]
Glo-
[D2]
69
Plain chant
Sic- ut lo- cu- tus est ad pa-tres no-stros, A- bra-ham et se- mi- ni e- jus in sae- cu- la.
[D3]
[HC]
[B]
[B.c.]
71
- ri- a Pa- tri, et Fi- li- o, et Fi- li-
et Fi- li- o, et Fi- li-
et Fi- li- o, et Fi- li-
et Fi- li-
et Fi- li- o, et Fi- li-

76
-o, et Spi- ri- tu- i san- cto, et Spi- ri-
-o, et Spi- ri-
-o, et Spi- ri- tu- i
-o, et Spi- ri- tu-
-o, et Spi- ri- tu-
82
-tu- i San- cto.
-tu- i San- cto.
San- cto.
-i San- cto.
-i San- cto.
Plain chant
84
Sic- ut e- rat in prin- ci- pi- o, et nunc, et sem- per, et in sae- cu- la sae- cu- lo- rum. A- men.

2. Magnificat (2)

11
me- a Do- mi- num.
me- a Do- mi- num.
me- a Do- mi- num.
me- a Do- mi- num.
me- a Do- mi- num.
13
Plain chant
Et ex- sul- ta- vit spi- ri- tus me- us in De- o sa- lu- ta- ri me- o.
14
[D1]
Qui- a re- spe- xit hu- mi- li- ta- tem an-
[D2]
[D3]
[BD]
Qui- a re- spe- xit hu- - mi- li- ta- tem an- cil- lae
[B]
Qui- a re- spe- xit, qui- a re- spe- xit hu- mi- li- ta- tem an- cil-
[B.c.]

19
-cil- lae su- ae:
ec- ce e- nim ex hoc be- a- tam me di- cent, me di-
ec- - ce e- nim ex hoc be- a- tam me di-
su- ae: ex hoc be- a- tam me di-
- lae su- ae: ec- ce e- nim ex hoc be- a- tam me di-
25
om- nes ge- ne- ra- ti- o- nes, ge-
-cent om- nes ge- ne-
-cent om- nes, om- nes ge- ne- ra- ti- o- nes, om- nes
-cent om- nes, om- nes ge- ne- ra-
-cent om- nes, om- nes ge- ne- ra- ti-

30
- ne- ra- ti- o- nes.
-ra- ti- o- nes.
ge- ne- ra- ti- o- nes.
- ti- o- nes.
-o- nes.
32
Plain chant
Qui- a fe- cit mi- hi ma- gna qui po- tens est: et san- ctum no- men e- jus.
33
[D1]
[D2]
ti-
[D3]
Et mi- se- ri- cor- di- a e- jus a pro- ge- ni- e in pro- ge- ni- es
[BD]
ti- men- ti-
[B]
ti-
[B.c.]

39
ti- men- ti- bus, ti- men- ti- bus, ti- men- ti- bus e- um.
-men- ti- bus, ti- men- - ti- bus, ti- men- ti- bus e- um.
ti- men- ti- bus_ e- um, ti-men- ti- bus, ti- men- ti- bus e- um.
-bus, ti- men- ti- bus e- um, ti- men- ti- bus e- um.
-men- ti- bus, ti- men- ti- bus, ti- men- ti- bus, ti- men- ti- bus e- um.
45
Plain chant
Fe- cit po- ten- ti- am in bra- chi- o su- o: di- sper- sit su- per- bos men- te cor- dis su- i.
46
[D1]
De- po- su- it po-
[D2]
[D3]
[BD]
[B]
[B.c.]

47
-ten- tes de se- de, et ex- al-
De- po- su- it po- ten- tes de se- de,
De- po- su- it po- ten- tes de se- de,
De- po- su- it po- ten- - tes de se- de,
De- po- su- it po- ten- tes de se- de,
52
-ta- - vit hu- mi- les,
et ex- al- ta- vit
et ex- al- ta- - vit
et ex- al- ta- vit, et ex- al-
et ex- al- ta- - vit hu- mi-

57
et ex- al- ta- vit hu- mi- les, hu- mi- les.
hu- mi- les, hu- - mi- les, hu- mi- les.
hu- mi- les, et ex- al- ta- - vit hu- mi- les.
-ta- vit hu- mi- les, et ex- al- ta- - - vit hu- mi- les.
-les, et ex- al- ta- - vit hu- mi- les.
62
Plain chant
E- su- ri- en- tes im- ple- vit bo- nis: et di- vi- tes di- mi- sit i- na- nes.
63
[D1]
Su-
[D2]
[D3]
[BD]
Su- sce- pit Is- ra-
[B]
[B.c.]

65
-sce- pit Is- - ra- el pu- - e- rum su- um,
Su- sce- pit Is- ra- el, su-
Su- sce- pit Is- ra- el,
-el, Is- ra- el, su- sce- - pit Is- ra- el, su- sce- pit Is-
Su- sce- pit Is- ra- el, su- sce- pit
70
su- sce- pit Is- ra- el pu- e- rum su- um,
-sce- pit Is- ra- el pu- e- rum su- um, pu- e- rum su- um,
Is- ra- el pu- e- rum su- um, pu- e- rum su- um,
- ra- el pu- e- rum su- um,
Is- ra- el pu- e- rum su- um, pu- e- rum su- um,

75
re- cor- da- - tus mi- se- ri- cor- di- ae___ su- ae,
re- cor-
re-
re- cor-
re- cor-
80
mi- se- ri- cor- - di- ae su- ae.
-da- tus, re- cor- da- tus mi- se- ri- cor- di- ae su- ae.
-cor- da- tus mi- se- ri- cor- di- ae su- ae, mi- se- - ri- cor- di- ae su ae.
-da- tus mi- se- ri- cor- - di- ae su- ae.
-da- tus mi- se- ri- cor- - di- ae su- ae.

85

Plain chant

Sic- ut lo- cu- tus est ad pa- tres no- stros, A- bra- ham et se- mi- ni e- jus in sae- cu- la.

86

[D1] Glo-

[D2]

[D3]

[BD]

[B] Glo-

[B.c.]

87

- ri- a Pa- tri, et Fi- li- o, et Fi- li- o, et___ Spi- ri-

Glo- ri- a Pa- tri, et Fi- li- o, et___ Spi- ri-

Glo- ri- a Pa- tri,___ et Fi- li- o, et Spi- ri-

Glo- - ri- a Pa- tri___ et Fi- li- o, et___ Spi- ri-

- ri- a Pa- tri et Fi- li- o, et___ Spi- ri-

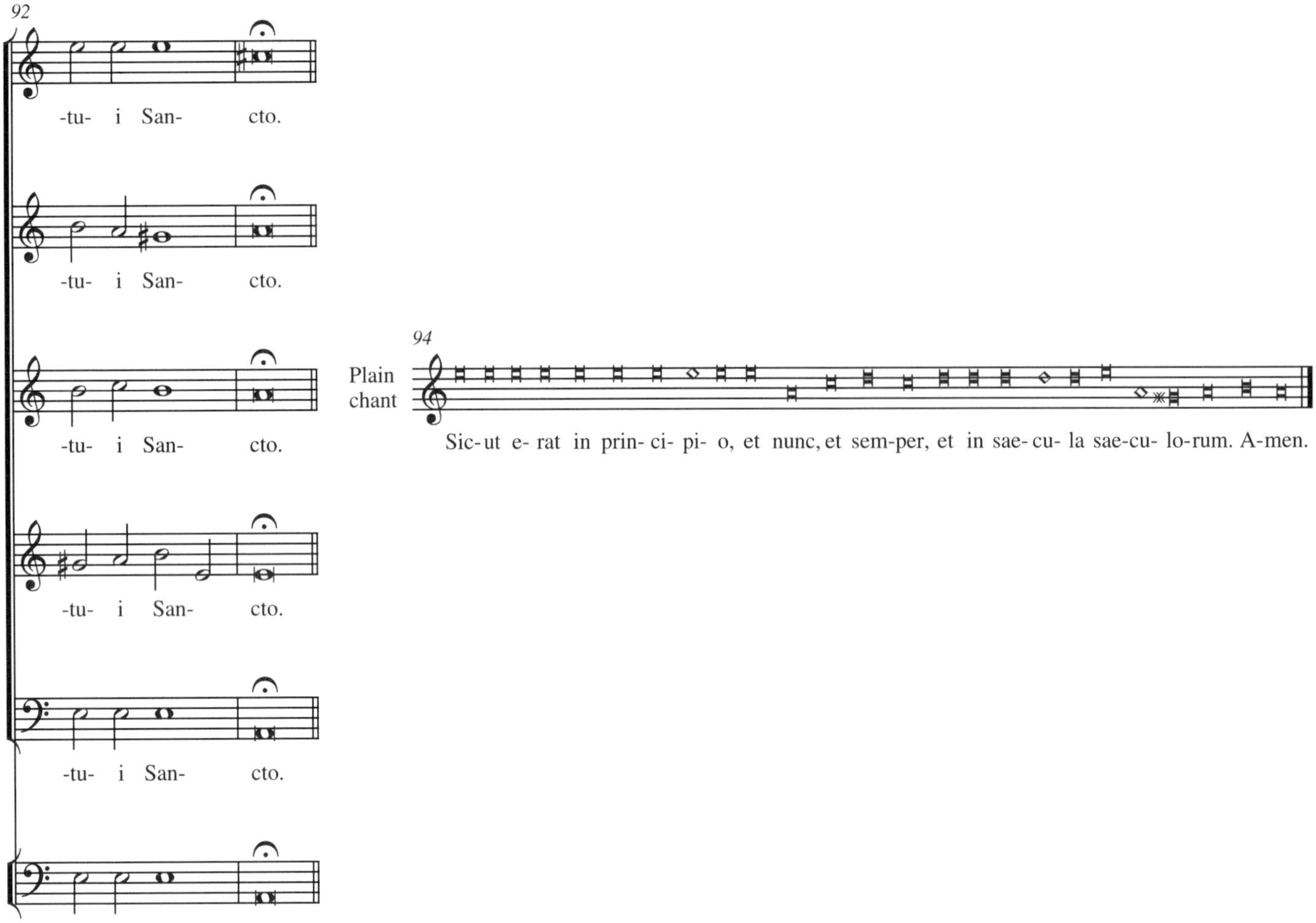

92
-tu- i San- cto.
-tu- i San- cto.
-tu- i San- cto.
-tu- i San- cto.
-tu- i San- cto.
94
Plain chant
Sic- ut e- rat in prin- ci- pi- o, et nunc, et sem-per, et in sae- cu- la sae-cu- lo-rum. A-men.

3. Magnificat (3)

[Dessus 1]
Ma- gni- fi- cat a- ni- ma, a- ni-ma me- a Do- mi-num,
[Dessus 2]
Ma- gni- fi- cat a- ni-
[Haute-contre]
Ma- gni- fi- cat a- ni-
[Basse]
Ma- gni- fi- cat a- ni-
[Basse continue]

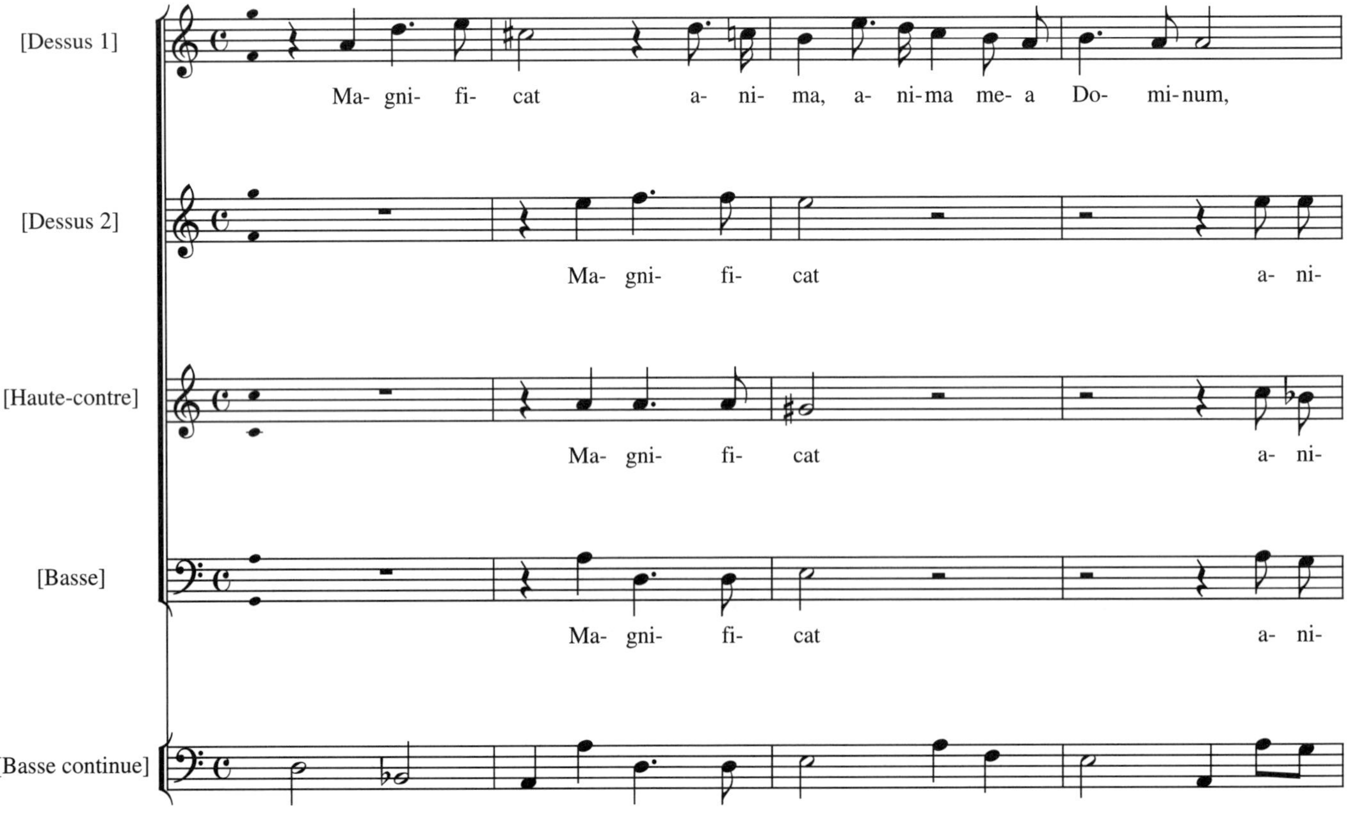

5
a- ni- ma, a- - ni- ma me- a Do- mi- num. Et
-ma me- a, a- ni- ma me- a Do- mi- num.
-ma me- a, a- ni- ma me- a Do- mi- num.
-ma me- a, a- ni- ma me- a Do- mi- num.
10
ex- sul- ta- vit spi- ri- tus me- us, spi- - ri- tus me- us
Et ex- sul- ta- vit spi- ri- tus me- us in De-
in De-
in De-
15
in De- o sa- lu- ta- ri me- o.
-o, in De- o sa- lu- ta- ri me- o, sa- lu- ta- ri me- o.
-o, in De- o sa- lu- ta- ri me- o.
-o, in De- o sa- lu- ta- ri me- o.

20
Qui- a re- spe- xit hu- mi- li- ta- tem an- cil- lae su-
Qui- a re- spe- xit hu- mi- li- ta- tem an- cil-
25
- ae: ec- ce e- nim ex hoc be- a- tam me di-
- lae su- ae: ec- ce e- nim ex hoc be- a- tam me di-
ec- ce e- nim ex hoc be- a- tam me di-
ec- ce e- nim ex hoc be- a- tam me di-
30
-cent om- nes ge- ne- ra- ti- o- nes. Qui- a fe-
-cent om- nes ge- ne- ra- - ti- o- nes.
-cent om- nes ge- ne- ra- - ti- o- nes.
-cent om- nes ge- ne ra- - ti- o- nes.

35
-cit mi- hi ma- gna qui po- tens est: et san- ctum
et san- ctum, et san- ctum
et san- ctum, et san- ctum
et san- ctum, et san- ctum
40
no- men e- jus. Et mi- se- ri- cor- di- a e- jus a pro- ge- ni-
no- men e- jus.
no- men e- jus.
no- men e- jus.
46
-e in pro- ge- ni- es ti- men- ti- bus e- um.
ti- men- ti- bus, ti- men- ti- bus e- um.
ti- men- ti- bus, ti- men- ti- bus e- um.
ti- men- ti- bus, ti- men- ti- bus e- um.

51
Fe- cit po- ten- ti- am in bra- chi- o su- o: di-
Fe- cit po- ten- ti- am in bra- chi- o su- o: di-
in bra- chi- o su- o: di-
di-
56
-sper- sit su- per- bos men- te cor- dis su- i, men- te cor- dis
-sper- sit su- per- bos men- te cor- dis su- i, men- te cor- dis
-sper- sit su- per- bos men- te cor- dis su- i, men- te cor- dis
-sper- sit su- per- bos men- te cor- dis su- i, men- te cor- dis
61
su- i, men- te cor- dis su- i.
su- i, men- te cor- dis su- i. De- po- su-
su- i, men- te cor- dis su- i.
su- i, men- te cor- dis su- i.

67
et ex- al- ta- - vit hu- mi- les, et ex- al- ta-
-it po- ten- tes de se- de, et ex- al- ta-
et ex- al- ta- vit, et ex- al- ta-
et ex- al- ta- vit, et ex- al- ta-
72
- vit hu- mi- les. E- su- ri- en- tes im- ple- vit
- vit hu- mi- les.
-vit hu- mi- les.
-vit hu- mi- les.
77
bo- nis: et di- vi- tes, et di- vi- tes di- mi- sit i- na- nes, et
et di- vi- tes, et di- vi- tes di- mi- sit i- na- nes, et
et di- vi- tes, et di- vi- tes di- mi- sit i- na- nes,
et di- vi- tes, et di- vi- tes di- mi- sit i- na- nes,

82
di- vi- tes, et di- vi- tes di- mi- sit i- na- nes.
di- vi- tes, et di- vi- tes di- mi- sit i- na- nes.
et di- vi- tes di- mi- sit i- na- nes.
et di- vi- tes di- mi- sit i- na- nes.
88
re-
Su- sce- pit Is- ra- el pu- e- rum su- um, re- cor- da-
re- cor- da-
re- cor-
93
-cor- da- tus mi- se- ri- cor- di- ae su- - ae.
-tus mi- se- ri- cor- di- ae, mi- se- ri- cor- di- ae su- ae.
-tus mi- se- ri- cor- di- ae, mi- se- ri- cor- - di- ae su- ae.
-da- tus mi- se- ri- cor- di- ae su- ae.

98
Sic- ut lo- cu- tus est ad pa- tres no- stros, ad pa- - tres no-
103
-stros, A- bra- ham et se- mi- ni e- jus in sae- cu- la, in sae- cu- la, in sae- cu-
A- bra- ham et se- mi- ni e- jus in sae- cu- la, in sae- cu- la, in sae- cu-
A- bra- ham et se- mi- ni e- jus in sae- cu- la, in sae- cu-
A- bra- ham et se- mi- ni e- jus in sae- cu- la, in sae- cu-
108
-la. Glo- - ri- a Pa- tri, et Fi- li- o, et Spi-
-la.
-la.
-la.

114
-ri- tu- i San- cto. Sic- ut e- rat in prin- ci- pi- o, et nunc,
Sic- ut e- rat in prin- ci- pi- o, et nunc,
Sic- ut e- rat in prin- ci- pi- o, et
Sic- ut e- rat in prin- ci- pi- o, et nunc,
120
et sem- per, et in sae- cu- la sae- cu- lo- rum, a- men, et in sae- cu-
et sem- per, et in sae- cu- la sae- cu- lo- rum, a- men, et in sae- cu-
nunc, et sem- per, et in sae- cu-
et sem- per, et in sae- cu-
125
-la sae- cu- lo- rum, a- - men, sae- cu- lo- rum. A- men.
-la sae- - cu- lo- rum, a- men, sae- cu- lo- rum. A- men.
-la sae- cu- lo- rum, a- men, sae- cu- lo- rum. A- men.
-la sae- cu- lo- rum, a- - men, sae- cu- lo- rum. A- men.

4. Magnificat (4)

16
[D1]
-spe- xit hu- mi- li- ta- tem, hu- mi- li- ta- tem an- cil-
[D2]
Qui- a re- spe- xit hu- mi- li- ta- tem, hu- mi- li- ta- tem an-
Org.
20
- lae su- ae: ec- ce e- nim ex hoc be- a- tam me di-
-cil- lae su- ae: ec- ce e- nim ex hoc be- a- tam me
25
-cent, me di- cent om- - nes ge- ne- ra- - ti- o-
di- cent om- nes ge- ne- ra- - ti- o- -
30
[D1]
-nes. Qui- a fe- cit mi- hi ma- gna qui po- tens est: et san-
[D2]
-nes. Qui- a fe- cit mi- hi ma- gna qui po- tens est: et san-
[BD]
Qui- a fe- cit mi- hi ma- gna qui po- tens est: et
[B]
Qui- a fe- cit mi- hi ma- gna qui po- tens est:
Org.

35
-ctum, et san- ctum no- men e- jus. Et mi- se- ri- cor- di-
-ctum, et san- ctum no- men e- jus.
san- ctum, et san- ctum no- men e- jus.
et san- ctum, et san- ctum no- men e- jus.
40
-a e- jus a pro- ge- ni- e in pro- ge- ni- es ti- men- ti- bus e-
45
-um. Fe- cit po- ten- ti- am in bra- chi- o su- o: di- sper-
Fe- cit, fe- cit po- ten- ti- am in bra- - chi- o su- o: di- sper-
Fe- cit po- ten- ti- am in bra- chi- o su- o: di- sper- sit
Fe- cit po- ten- ti- am in bra- chi- o su- o: di-

50
-sit su- per- bos men- te cor- dis su- i.
-sit su- per- bos men- te cor- dis sui- i. De- po- su- it po- ten-
su- per- bos men- te cor- dis su- i.
-sper- sit su- per- bos men- te cor- dis su- i.
55
et ex- al- ta- - - vit hu- mi- les. E- su- ri-
-tes de se- de, et ex- al- ta- - vit hu- mi- les. E- su- ri-
E- su- ri-
E- su- ri-
60
-en- tes im- ple- vit bo- nis: et di- vi- tes di- mi- sit
-en- tes im- - ple- vit bo- nis: et di- vi- tes di- mi- - sit i- na-
-en- tes im- ple- vit bo- nis:
-en- tes im- ple- vit bo- nis:

65
— i- na- nes, di- mi- sit i- na- nes. Su- sce- pit Is- ra- el pu-
-nes, i- na- nes, di- mi- sit i- na- nes.
di- mi- sit i- na- nes.
di- mi- sit i- na- nes.
71
-e- rum su- um, re- cor- da- tus mi- se- ri- cor- di- ae su-
mi- se- ri- cor- di- ae su-
76
-ae. Sic- ut lo- cu- tus est ad pa- tres no- stros, A-
-ae. Sic- ut lo- cu- tus, lo- cu- tus est ad pa- tres no- stros, A-
Sic- ut lo- cu- tus est ad pa- tres no- stros, A-
Sic- ut lo- cu- tus est ad pa- tres no- stros, A-

81
- bra-ham et se- mi- ni e- jus, e- jus in saе- cu- la, in sae- cu- la, in sae- cu-
- bra-ham et se- mi- ni e- jus in saе- cu- la, in sae- cu- la, in sae- cu-
- bra-ham et se- mi- ni e- jus, e- jus in sae- cu- la, in sae- cu-
- bra-ham et se- mi- ni e- jus, e- jus in sae- cu- la, in sae- cu-
86
-la. Glo- - ri- a, glo- - ri- a Pa- tri, et Fi- li-
-la.
-la.
-la.
91
-o, et Spi- ri- tu- i San- cto. Sic- ut e- rat
Sic- ut e- rat
Sic- ut e- rat
Sic- ut e- rat

96
in prin- ci- pi- o, et nunc, et sem- per, et in sae- cu- la, et in sae- cu-
in prin- ci- pi- o, et nunc, et sem- per, et in sae- cu- la, et in sae- cu-
in prin- ci- pi- o, et nunc, et sem- per, et in sae- cu-
in prin- ci- pi- o, et nunc, et sem- per, et in sae- cu-
101
-la sae- cu- lo- rum. A- men, a- men.
-la sae- cu- lo- - rum. A- men, a- - men.
-la sae- cu- lo- rum. A- men, a- men.
-la sae- cu- lo- rum. A- men, a- men.

5. Magnificat (5)

13
hu- mi- li- ta- tem an- cil- lae su- ae: ec- ce e- nim ex hoc be-
-mi- li- ta- - tem an- cil- lae su- ae: ec- ce e- nim ex hoc be-
-mi- li- ta- - tem an- cil- lae su- ae: ec- ce e- nim ex hoc be-
-mi- li- ta- - tem an- cil- lae su- ae: ec- ce e- nim ex hoc be-
19
-a- tam me di- cent om- nes ge- ne-
-a- tam me di- cent om- nes
-a- tam me di- cent om- - nes, om- - nes ge- ne-
-a- tam me di- cent om- nes, om- nes ge- ne-
24
-ra- ti- o- nes.
ge- ne- ra- ti- o- nes.
-ra- ti- o- nes.
-ra- ti- o- nes.
26
Plain chant
Qui- a fe- cit mi- hi ma- gna qui po- tens est: et san- ctum no- men e- jus.

27
[D1]
[D2]
[BD]
[B]
Org.
Et mi- se- ri- cor- di- a e- jus a pro- ge- ni- e in pro- ge- ni- es
Et mi- se- ri- cor- di- a e- jus a pro- ge- ni- e in pro- ge- ni- es
Et mi- se- ri- cor- di- a e- jus a pro- ge- ni- e in pro- ge- ni- es ti-
Et mi- se- ri- cor- di- a e- jus a pro- ge- ni- e in pro- ge- ni- es
32
ti- men- ti- bus e- um, ti- men- ti- bus, ti- men- ti- bus, ti-
ti- men- - ti- bus e- um, ti- men- ti-
-men- ti- bus e- - um, ti- men- ti- bus e- um, ti- men-
ti- men- ti- bus e- um, ti- men- ti-
37
-men- ti- bus e- um.
-bus e- um.
-ti- bus e- um.
-bus e- um.
39
Plain chant
Fe- cit po- ten- ti- am in bra- chi- o su- o: di- sper- sit su- per- bos men- te cor- dis su- i.

40
[D1]
De- po- su- it, de- po- su- it po- ten- tes de se- de, et
[D2]
De- po- su- it, de- po- su- it po- ten- tes de se- de,
[BD]
De- po- su- it, de- po- su- it po- ten- tes de se- de,
[B]
De- po- su- it po- ten- tes de se- de,
Org.
45
ex- al- ta- - vit hu- mi- les, et ex- al- ta- - vit, et
et ex- al- ta- - vit, et ex- al- ta- vit
et ex- al- ta- vit, et ex- al- ta- vit, et ex- al- ta- vit, et ex- al-
et ex- al- ta- vit, et ex- al- ta-
50
ex- al- ta- vit hu- mi- les.
hu- mi- les, hu- mi- les.
-ta- vit hu- mi- les.
- vit hu- mi- les.
52
Plain chant
E- su- ri- en- tes im- ple- vit bo- nis: et di- vi- tes di- mi- sit i- na- nes.

53
[D1]
Su- sce- pit Is- ra- el, Is- - ra- el pu- e- rum su- um,
[D2]
Su- sce-
[BD]
Su- sce- pit Is- ra- el, Is- ra- el pu- e- rum su- um,
[B]
Su- sce- pit
Org.
58
pu- e- rum su- um, re- cor- da- tus mi-
-pit Is- ra- el pu- e- rum su- um, re- cor- da- tus mi- se- ri-
Is- ra- el pu- - e- rum su- um, re- cor- da- tus mi- se- ri-
Is- ra- el pu- e- rum su- um, re- cor-
63
-se- ri- cor- - di- ae, mi- se- ri- cor- di-
-cor- di- ae su- ae, mi- se- ri- cor- di- ae, mi- se- ri- cor- di-
-cor- - - di- ae, mi- se- ri- cor- di- ae, mi- se- ri-
-da- tus mi- se- ri- cor- di- ae su- ae, mi- se- ri- cor- di-

68
-ae su- ae.
-ae su- ae.
-cor- di- ae su- ae.
-ae su- ae.
Plain chant
70
Sic-ut lo- cu-tus est ad pa- tres no-stros, A- bra-ham et se- mi- ni e- jus in sae-cu- la.
71
[D1]
Glo- ri- a Pa- - tri, et Fi- li- o, Pa- tri, et
[D2]
Glo- ri- a Pa- tri, et Fi- li- o, Pa- tri, et
[BD]
Glo- ri- a Pa- tri, et Fi- li- o, Pa- tri, et Fi-
[B]
Glo- ri- a Pa- tri, et Fi-
Org.
78
Fi- li- o, et Spi- ri- - - tu- i San-
Fi- li- o, et Spi- ri- - - tu- i San-
- li- o, et Spi- ri- tu- i
- li- o, et Spi- ri- - tu- i San-

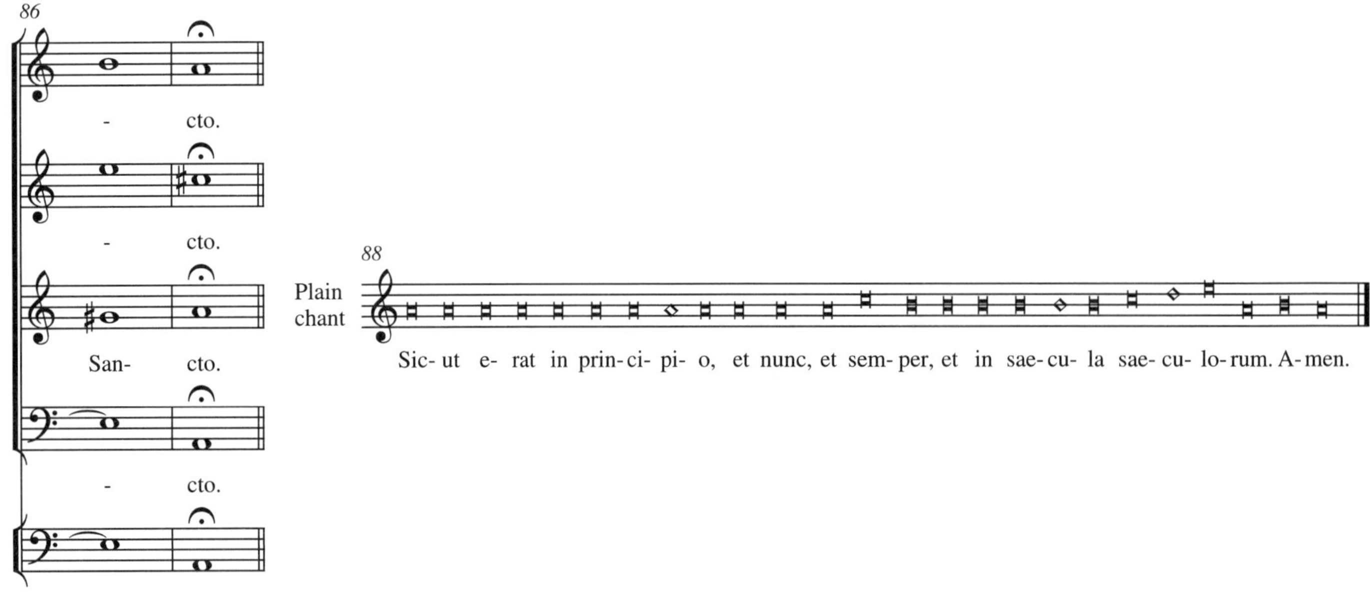

6. Magnificat (6)

14
[D1]
Qui- a re- spe- xit hu- mi- li- ta- tem an- cil- lae su- ae: ec- ce
Org.
20
e- nim ex hoc be- a- tam me di- cent om- nes ge- ne- ra- - ti- o- nes.
27
[D1]
Qui- a fe- cit mi- hi ma- gna qui po- tens est: et
[D2]
Qui- a fe- cit mi- hi ma- gna qui po- tens est: et
[HC]
Qui- a fe- - cit mi- - hi ma- gna qui po- tens est:
[B]
Qui- a fe- - cit mi- hi ma- gna qui po- tens est: et
Org.
32
san- ctum no- men e- jus. Et mi-
san- ctum no- men e- - jus. Et mi- se- ri- cor- di-
et san- - ctum no- men e- jus.
san- ctum no- men e- jus.

39
[D1]
-se- ri- cor- di- a e- jus a pro- ge- ni- e in pro- ge- ni-
[D2]
-a e- - jus a pro- ge- ni- e, a pro- ge- ni-
Org.
45
-es, in pro- ge- ni- es ti-men-ti- bus e- - - um.
-e in pro- ge- ni- es: ti- men- ti- bus ti- men- ti- bus e- - um.
52
[D1]
Fe- cit po- ten- ti- am in bra- chi- o su- o: di- sper- sit su- per- bos men- te cor- dis
[D2]
Fe- cit po- ten- ti- am in bra- chi- o su- o: di- sper- sit su- per- bos
[HC]
Fe- cit po- ten- ti- am in bra- chi- o su- o: di- sper- sit su- per-
[B]
Fe- cit po- ten- ti- am in bra- chi- o su- o: di- sper- sit su- per- bos
Org.
57
su- i, men- te cor- dis su- i. De- po- su- it po- ten- tes de
men- te cor- - dis su- i.
-bos men- te cor- dis su- i.
men- te cor- dis su- i.

63
[D1]
se- de, et ex- al- ta- vit hu- mi- les, et ex- al- ta- vit
Org.
71
[D1]
hu- mi- les. E- su- ri- en- tes im- ple- vit bo- nis: et di- vi-
[D2]
E- su- ri- en- tes im- ple- vit bo- nis: et di-
[HC]
E- su- ri- en- tes im- ple- vit bo- - nis: et di- vi-
[B]
E- su- ri- en- tes im- ple- vit bo- nis: et di- vi-
Org.
77
-tes di- mi- - sit i- na- nes, di- mi- sit i- na- - nes.
- vi- tes di- mi- sit i- na- nes, di- mi- sit i- na- nes.
-tes di- mi- sit i- na- nes, di- mi- - sit i- na- nes.
-tes di- mi- sit i- na- nes, di- mi- sit i- na- nes.
83
[D1]
Su- sce- pit Is- ra- el pu- e- rum su- um, re- cor-
[D2]
Su- sce- pit Is- ra- el pu- e- rum su- um, re- cor- da- tus,
Org.

89
-da- tus, re- cor- da- tus mi- se- ri- cor- di- ae su- ae.
re- cor- da- tus mi- se- ri- cor- di- ae su- - - ae.
97
[D1]
Sic- ut lo- cu- tus est ad pa- tres no- stros, A- bra- ham, A- bra-
[D2]
Sic- ut lo- cu- tus est ad pa- tres no- stros, A- bra- ham, A- bra- ham
[HC]
Sic- ut lo- cu- tus est ad pa- tres no- stros, A- bra- ham, A- bra- ham et
[B]
Sic- ut lo- cu- tus est ad pa- tres no- stros, A- bra- ham, A- bra- ham et
Org.
102
-ham et se- mi- ni e- jus in sae- cu- la.
et se- mi- ni e- jus in sae- cu- la. et Fi- li-
se- mi- ni e- jus in sae- cu- la.
se- mi- ni e- - jus in sae- cu- la. Glo- ri- a Pa- tri,

109
et Spi- ri- tu- i San- cto. Sic- ut e- rat in prin- ci- pi- o,
-o, Sic- ut e- rat in prin- ci- pi- o,
Sic- ut e- - rat in prin- ci- pi-
Sic- ut e- rat in prin- ci- pi- o,
116
et nunc, et sem- per, et in sae- cu- la sae- cu- lo- rum, a-
et nunc, et sem- per,
-o, et nunc, et sem- per,
et nunc, et sem- per,
124
-men, et in sae- cu- la sae- - cu- lo- rum. A- men.
et in sae- cu- la sae- cu- lo- rum. A- - men.
et in sae- cu- la sae- cu- lo- rum. A- men.
et in sae- cu- la sae- cu- lo- rum. A- men.

7. Te Deum (1)

[Dessus]
[Haute-contre]
[Haute-taille]
[Basse]
Orgue
Te De- um lau- da- mus: te Do- mi- num con- fi- te- mur.
6
Te ae- ter- num Pa- trem om- nis ter- ra ve- ne- ra- tur. Ti- bi
Te ae- ter- num Pa- trem om- nis ter- ra ve- ne- ra- tur.
Te ae- ter- num Pa- trem om- nis ter- ra ve- ne- ra- tur. Ti-
Te ae- ter- num Pa- trem om- nis ter- ra ve- ne- ra- tur.
10
om- nes An- ge- li, ti- bi Cae- li et u- ni- ver-
- bi om- nes An- - ge- li, ti- bi Cae- li et u- ni-

15
-sae Po- tes- ta- - tes: Ti- bi Che- ru-bim et Se- ra- phim in- ces- sa- bi- li vo-
Ti- bi Che- ru- bim et Se- ra- phim in- ces- sa- bi- li vo-
-ver- sae Po- tes- ta- tes: Ti- bi Che- ru- bim et Se- ra- phim in- ces- sa- bi- li vo- ce
Ti- bi Che- ru- bim et Se- ra- phim in- ces- sa- bi- li vo-
20
- ce pro- cla- - mant: San- - - ctus:
-ce pro- cla- mant: San- -
pro- cla- mant: San- - - ctus: San-
-ce pro- cla- mant: San- -
27
San- ctus: San- - - ctus: San- -
-ctus: San- - ctus: San- - - ctus:
- - - - - ctus: San- ctus:
-ctus: San- - - - ctus: San-

34
- - ctus Do- mi- nus De- us Sa- ba-
San- ctus: San- ctus Do- mi- nus De- us Sa- ba-
San- - ctus Do- mi- nus De- us Sa- ba-
- - ctus Do- mi- nus De- us Sa- ba-
40
-oth. Ple- ni sunt cae- li et ter-
-oth. Ple- ni sunt cae- li et ter- ra, ple- ni sunt cae- li et
-oth. Ple- ni sunt cae- li, ple- ni sunt cae- li, ple- ni sunt cae- li et
-oth. Ple- ni sunt cae- li, ple- ni sunt cae- li et ter-
45
-ra ma- je- sta- tis glo- - ri- ae tu- ae, glo- ri- ae tu- ae. Te glo- ri-
ter- ra ma- je- sta- tis glo- - ri- ae tu- ae, glo- ri- ae tu- ae.
ter- ra ma- je- sta- tis glo- - ri- ae tu- ae, glo- ri- ae tu- ae.
-ra ma- je- sta- tis glo- - ri- ae tu- ae, glo- ri- ae tu- ae.

51
-o- sus A- po- sto- lo- rum cho- rus: Te Pro- phe- ta- rum lau- da- bi-
Te Pro- phe- ta- rum lau-
Te Pro- phe- ta- rum lau- da- bi-
Te Pro- phe- ta- rum lau- da- bi-
56
-lis nu- me- rus: Te Mar- ty- rum can- di- da- tus lau- dat
-da- bi- lis nu- me- rus:
-lis nu- me- rus: Te Mar- ty- rum can- di- da- tus lau- dat, lau-
-lis nu- me- rus:
61
ex- er- ci- tus. Te per or- bem ter- ra- rum san- - cta
Te per or- bem ter- ra- rum san- - cta
- dat ex- er- ci- tus. Te per or- bem ter- - ra- - rum san-
Te per or- bem ter- ra- rum san- cta

68
con- fi- te- - tur Ec- cle- - si- a: Pa-
con- fi- te- - - tur Ec- cle- si- a:
-cta con- fi- te- - tur Ec- cle- si- a:
con- fi- te- - tur Ec- cle- si- a:
75
-trem im- men- sae ma- je- sta- - tis: Ve- ne- ran- dum tu- um ve- rum, et u- ni- cum
Ve- ne- ran- dum tu- um ve- rum, et u- ni-
Pa- trem im- men- sae ma- je- sta- tis: Ve- ne- ran- dum tu- um ve- rum, et u- ni- cum Fi-
Ve- ne- ran- dum tu- um ve- rum, et u- ni- cum
80
Fi- li- um: Sanc- tum quo- que, san- ctum quo- que Pa- ra-
-cum Fi- li- um: Sanc- tum quo- que, san- ctum quo- que Pa-
- li- um: Sanc- tum quo- que, san- ctum quo- que Pa- ra- cli-
Fi- li- um: Sanc- tum quo- que, san- ctum quo- que Pa- ra- cli-

84
-cli-tum Spi- ri- tum. Tu Rex glo- ri- ae, Chri- ste. Tu Pa- tris sem- pi- ter- nus es
-ra- cli-tum Spi- ri- tum.
tum Spi- ri- tum.
-tum Spi- ri- tum.
90
Fi- li- us, es Fi- li- us, Fi- li- us. Tu ad li- be- ran- dum su- sce- ptu- rus ho- mi-
Tu ad li- be- ran- dum su- sce- ptu- rus ho- mi-
Tu ad li- be- ran- dum su- sce- ptu- rus ho- mi-
Tu ad li- be- ran- dum su- sce- ptu- rus ho- mi-
95
-nem, non hor- ru- i- sti Vir- gi- nis u- te- rum, Vir- gi- nis u- te- rum.
-nem, non hor- ru- i- sti Vir- gi- nis u- te- rum, Vir- gi- nis u- te- rum.
-nem, non hor- ru- i- sti Vir- gi- nis u- te- rum, Vir- gi- nis u- te- rum. Tu de- vi- cto mor- tis a- cu- le-
-nem, non hor- ru- i- sti Vir- gi- nis u- te- rum, Vir- gi- nis u- te- rum.

100
Tu ad de- xte-
-o, a- pe- ru- i- sti cre- den- ti- bus re- - gna cae- lo- rum. Tu ad de- xte-
Tu ad de- xte-
105
Tu ad de- xte-ram, tu ad de- xte- ram De- i se- des, in glo- - ri- a Pa-
-ram, tu ad de- xte- ram, tu ad de- xte- ram De- i se- des, in glo- - ri- a Pa-
-ram, tu ad de- xte- ram De- i se- des, in glo- ri- a Pa-
-ram, tu ad de- xte- ram De- i se- des, in glo- ri- a Pa-
110
-tris. Ju- dex cre- de- ris es- se, es- - se ven- tu- -
-tris. Ju- dex cre- de- ris es- se, es- se ven- tu-
-tris. Ju- dex cre- de- ris es- se, es- se ven- tu-
-tris. Ju- dex cre- de- ris es- se ven- tu- -

117
-rus. Te er- go quae- su- mus, quae- su- mus, tu-
-rus. Te er- go quae- su- mus, tu- is
-rus. Te er- go quae- su- mus, tu- is
-rus. Te er- go quae- su- mus, tu- is
125
-is fa- - mu- lis sub- - ve- ni, quos pre- ti- o-
fa- mu- lis sub- - - ve- ni, quos pre- ti-
fa- mu- lis sub- - ve- ni, quos pre- ti-
fa- mu- lis sub- - ve- ni, quos pre- ti-
132
- so san- gui- ne re- de- mi- sti.
-o- so san- gui- ne re- de- mi- - sti.
-o- - so san- gui- ne re- - de- mi- sti.
-o- so san- - gui- ne re- de- mi- sti.

139
Ae- ter- na fac cum san- ctis tu- is in glo- ri- a nu- me- ra- ri. Sal- vum
Sal- vum
Sal- vum
Sal- vum
144
fac po- pu- lum tu- um Do- mi- ne, et be- ne- dic he- re-
fac po- pu- lum tu- um Do- mi- ne, et be- ne- dic he- re- di-
fac po- - pu- lum tu- um Do- mi- ne, et be- ne- dic he- re- di- ta- ti
fac po- pu- lum tu- um Do- mi- ne, et be- ne- dic he- re- di- ta- ti
149
- di- ta- ti tu- ae. Et re- ge e- os, et re- ge e- os, et ex- tol- le
-ta- ti tu- ae.
tu- ae. Et re- ge e- os, et re- ge e- os, et ex-
tu- ae.

155
il- los us- que in ae- ter- num. Per sin- - gu- los di- es,
Per sin- - gu- los di-
-tol- le il- los us- que in ae- ter- num. Per sin- - gu- los di-
Per sin- - gu- los di- es,
160
be- ne- di- - ci- mus te. Et lau- da- mus no- men tu- um in
-es, be- ne- di- - ci- mus te. Et lau- da- mus no- men tu- um in
-es, be- ne- di- ci- mus te. Et lau- da- mus in
be- ne- di- - ci- mus te. Et lau- da- mus no- men tu- um in
164
sae- cu- lum sae- - cu- li. Di- gna- re Do- mi- ne di- - e i- sto si- ne pec-
sae- cu-lum sae- - cu- li.
sae- cu- lum sae- cu- li.
sae- cu- lum sae- - cu- li.

170
-ca- to nos cu- sto- di- re. Mi- se- re- re no- - stri
Mi- se- re- re no- - stri
Mi- se- re- re no- stri
Mi- se- re- re no- stri
176
Do- mi- ne, mi- se- re- re no- stri Do- mi- ne,
Do- mi- ne, mi- se- re- re no- stri Do- mi- ne,
Do- mi- ne, mi- se- re- re no- stri Do- mi- ne,
Do- mi- ne, mi- se- re- re no- stri Do- mi- ne,
184
mi- - se- re- - re no- stri. Fi- at mi- se- ri-
mi- se- re- - re no- stri.
mi- se- re- re no- - stri.
mi- se- re- re no- - stri.

191
-cor- di- a tu- a Do- mi- ne su- per nos, quem- ad- mo-dum, quem- ad- mo- dum spe-
196
-ra- vi- mus in te. In te Do- mi- ne spe- ra- vi, in te Do- mi- ne spe- ra-
In te Do- mi- ne spe- ra- vi, in te Do- mi- ne spe- ra-
In te Do- mi- ne spe- ra- vi, in te Do- mi- ne spe- ra-
In te Do- mi- ne spe- ra- vi, in te Do- mi- ne spe- ra-
202
-vi: non con- fun- - dar, non con- fun- dar in ae- ter-
- vi: non con- fun- - - dar, non con-
-vi: non con- fun- - dar in ae- ter- num, in ae-
-vi: non con- fun- dar, non con- fun- dar, non con-

210
- num, non con- fun- dar in ae- ter- - num.
-fun- - dar in ae- ter- - num.
-ter- num, in ae- ter- - num, in ae- ter- num.
-fun- dar in ae- ter- - num.

8. Te Deum (2)

[Dessus 1]
[Dessus 2]
[Bas-dessus]
[Basse]
Orgue
Te De- um lau- da-
Te De- - um lau- - da- -
Te De- - um lau- da- mus:
Te De- um lau- da- -

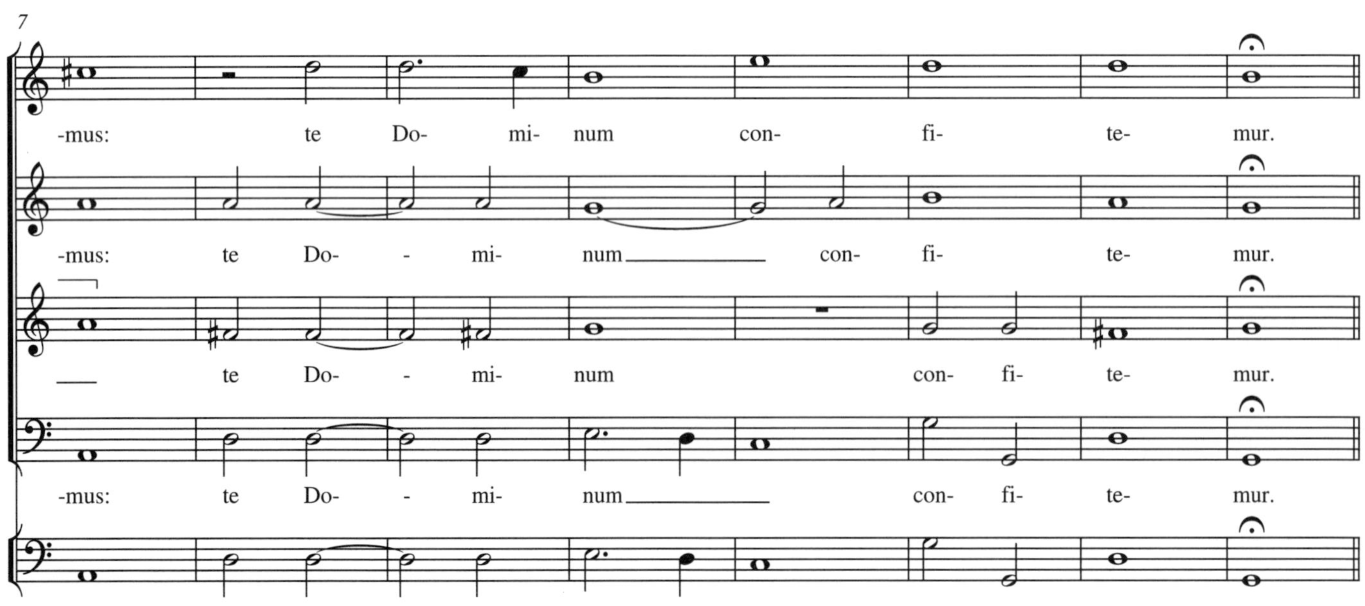
7
-mus: te Do- mi- num con- fi- te- mur.
-mus: te Do- - mi- num con- fi- te- mur.
te Do- - mi- num con- fi- te- mur.
-mus: te Do- - mi- num con- fi- te- mur.

15
Plain chant
Tc ae- ter- num Pa- trem om- nis ter- ra ve- ne- ra- tur.
16
[D1]
Ti- bi om- nes
[D2]
Ti- bi om- nes
[BD]
Ti- bi om- nes
[B]
Ti- bi om- nes
Org.
(16)
An- ge- li, ti- bi Cae- li et u- ni- ver- - sae Po- tes-
An- ge- li, ti- bi Cae- li et u- ni- ver- sae Po- tes-
An- ge- li, ti- bi Cae- li et u- ni- ver- sae Po- - tes-
An- ge- li, ti- bi Cae- li et u- ni- ver- sae Po- - tes-
20
-ta- tes:
-ta- tes:
-ta- tes:
-ta- tes:
22
Plain chant
Ti- bi Che- ru- bim et Se- ra-phim in- ces- sa- bi- li vo- ce pro- cla- mant:

23
[D1]
San- - - - - ctus:
[D2]
San- - - - - - ctus: San- -
[BD]
San- - - ctus: San- - ctus: San-
[B]
San- - - ctus:
Org.
32
San- - - ctus: San- -
- - ctus: San- ctus: San- - ctus:
- - - ctus: San- -
San- - - ctus: San- - - -
39
- ctus: Do- mi- nus De- us Sa- ba- oth.
San- - ctus: Do- mi- nus De- us Sa- ba- oth.
- ctus: Do- mi- nus De- us Sa- ba- oth.
- ctus: Do- mi- nus De- us Sa- ba- oth.

43
Plain chant
Ple- ni sunt cae- li et ter- ra ma- je- sta- tis glo- ri- ae tu- ae.
44
[D1]
Te
[D2]
Te
[BD]
Te
[B]
Te
Org.
46
glo- ri- o- sus A- po- sto- lo- - - rum
glo- ri- o- sus A- po- sto- lo-
glo- ri- o- sus A- po- sto- lo- - rum cho-
glo- ri- o- sus A- po- sto- lo- rum cho- -
53
cho- - rus.
- rum cho- rus.
- - rus.
- - rus.
56
Plain chant
Te Pro- phe- ta- rum lau- da- bi- lis nu- me- rus:

57
[D1]
Te Mar- ty- rum can- di- da- tus lau- - dat ex- er- ci- tus.
[D2]
Te Mar- ty- rum can- di- da- tus lau- dat ex- - er- ci- tus.
[BD]
lau- dat ex- er- ci- tus.
[B]
lau- dat ex- er- ci- tus.
Org.
63
Plain chant
Te per or- bem ter- ra- rum san- cta con- fi- te- tur Ec- cle- si- a:
64
[D1]
[D2]
Pa- -
[BD]
Pa- trem,
[B]
Pa- -
Org.
66
Pa- - - trem im- men- sae ma- je- sta- tis:
- trem im- men- sae ma- je- sta- tis:
Pa- trem im- men- sae ma- je- - sta- tis:
- trem im- men- sae ma- - je- sta- tis:

74
Plain chant
Ve- ne- ran- dum tu- um ve- rum, et u- ni- cum Fi- li- um:
75
[D1]
San- - ctum quo-
[D2]
San- ctum quo-
[BD]
San- - ctum quo-
[B]
San- ctum quo-
Org.
78
-que Pa- ra- cli- tum, Pa- ra- cli- - tum Spi- ri- tum, Spi- ri- tum.
-que Pa- - ra- - cli- tum Spi- - - ri- tum.
- que Pa- ra- cli- - tum Spi- ri- tum.
-que Pa- ra- cli- - - tum Spi- ri- tum, Spi- ri- tum.
87
Plain chant
Tu Rex glo- ri- ae Chri- ste.
88
[D1]
Tu Pa- - tris sem- pi-
[D2]
Tu Pa- tris sem- - pi-
[BD]
Tu Pa- tris sem- pi- ter- nus,
[B]
Tu Pa- - tris sem- pi-
Org.

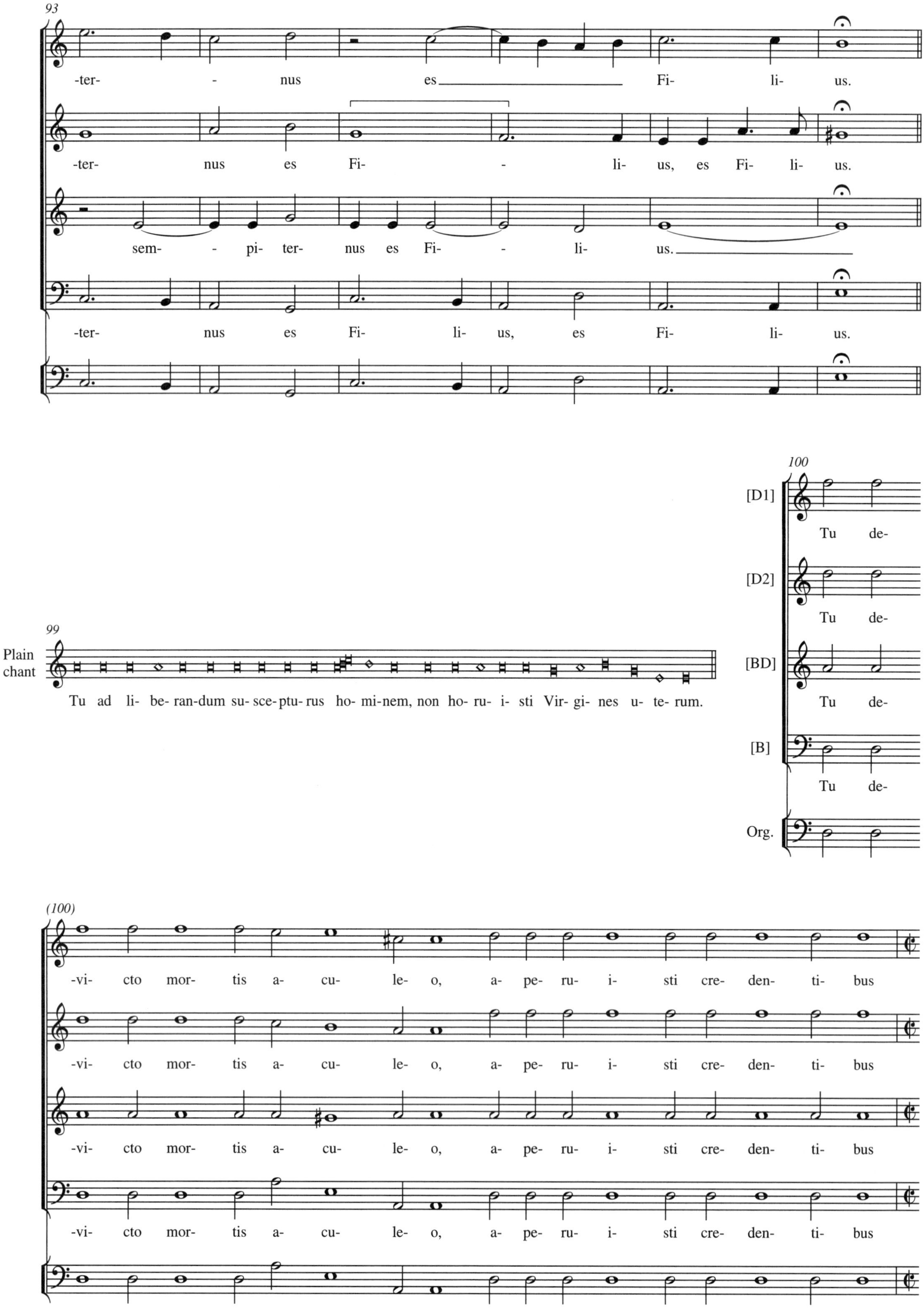

93

-ter- - nus es Fi- li- us.

-ter- nus es Fi- - li- us, es Fi- li- us.

sem- - pi- ter- nus es Fi- - li- us.

-ter- nus es Fi- li- us, es Fi- li- us.

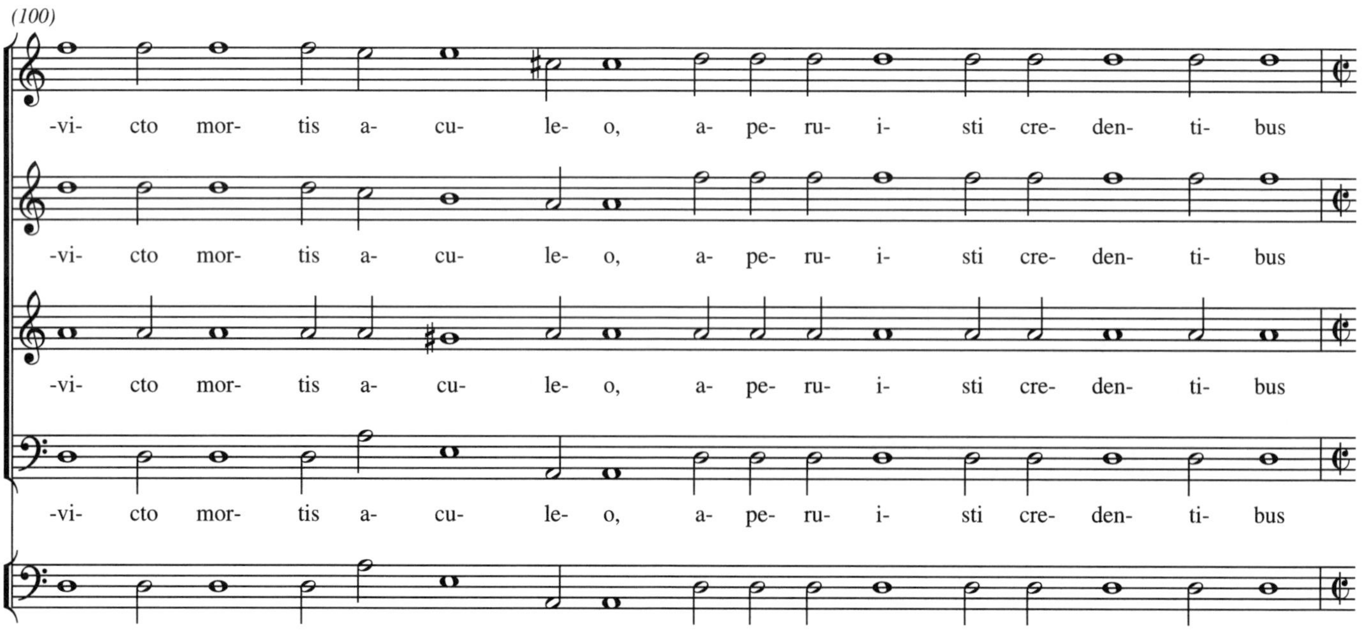

101
re- - gna caelo- rum, cae- lo- rum.
re- gna cae- lo- - rum, cae- lo- rum.
re- - gna cae- lo- rum, cae- lo- rum.
re- - gna cae- lo- - - rum.
108
Plain chant
Tu ad de- xte- ram De- i se- des, in glo- ri- a Pa- tris.
109
[D1]
Ju- dex cre- de- ris es-
[D2]
Ju- dex cre- de- ris es-
[BD]
Ju- dex cre- de- ris es-
[B]
Ju- dex cre- de- ris es-
Org.
111
- se ven- tu- rus, ven- tu- rus.
-se ven- tu- rus, ven- tu- rus.
-se ven- - - tu- rus, ven- tu- rus.
-se ven- - tu- rus, ven- - tu- rus.
117
Plain chant
Te er- go quae- su- mus tu- is fa- mu- lis sub- ven- i, quos pre- ti- o- so san- gui- ne re- de- mi- sti.

118
[D1]
Ae- ter- - na fac cum san- ctis
[D2]
Ae- ter- - na fac, ae- ter- - na fac cum san- ctis tu- is in
[BD]
cum san- ctis tu- is in
[B]
Ae- ter- na fac cum san- ctis tu- is
Org.
126
tu- is in glo- ri- a nu- - me- ra- ri.
glo- ri- a, in glo- ri- a nu- me- ra- ri.
glo- ri- a nu- - - me- ra- - - ri.
in glo- ri- a, glo- ri- a nu- - me- ra- ri.
134
Plain chant
Sal- vum fac po- pu- lum tu- um Do- mi- ne, et be- ne- dic he- re- di- ta- ti tu- ae.
135
[D1]
Et re- ge
[D2]
Et re- ge
[BD]
[B]
Et re- ge
Org.

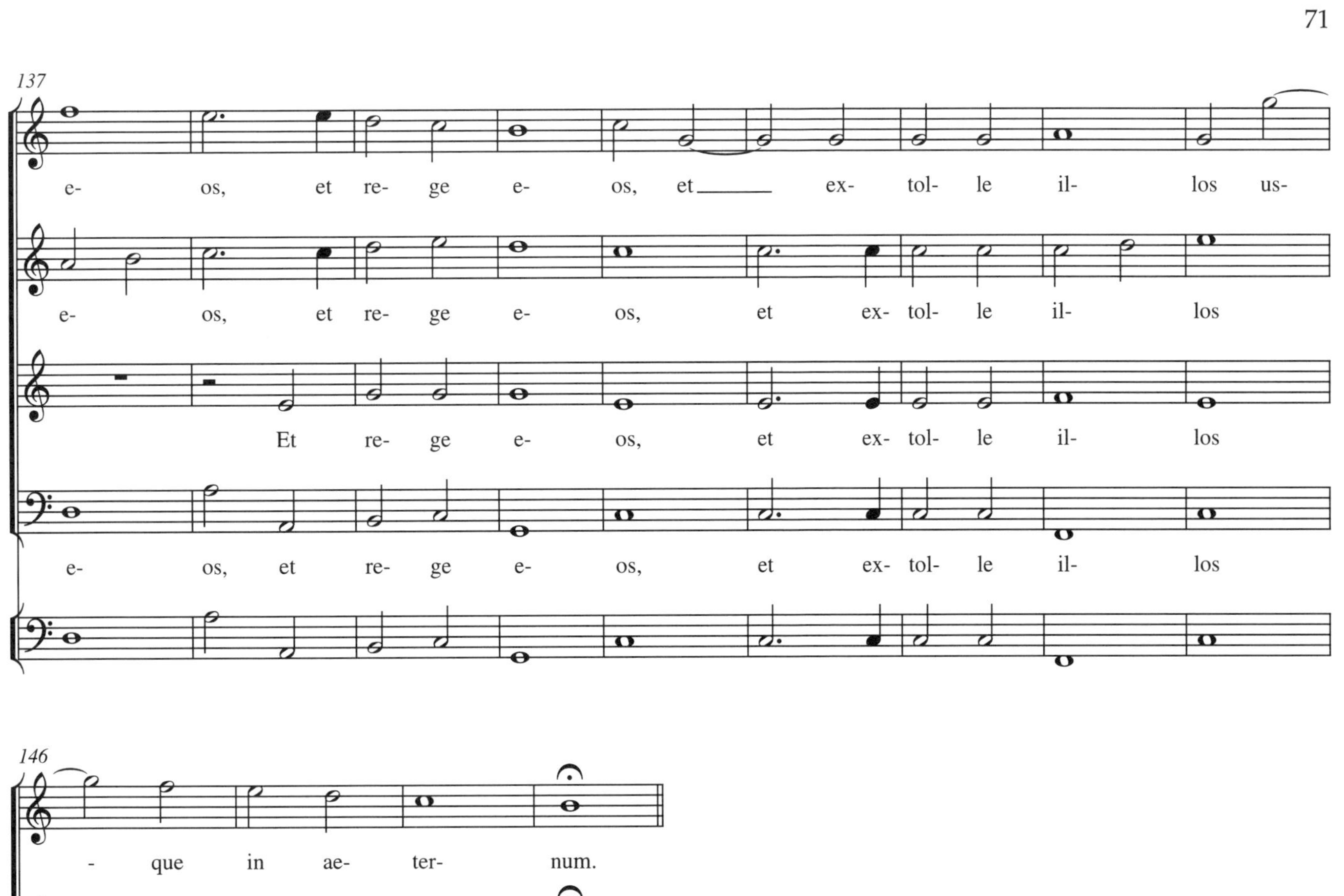
137
e- os, et re- ge e- os, et ex- tol- le il- los us-
e- os, et re- ge e- os, et ex- tol- le il- los
Et re- ge e- os, et ex- tol- le il- los
e- os, et re- ge e- os, et ex- tol- le il- los

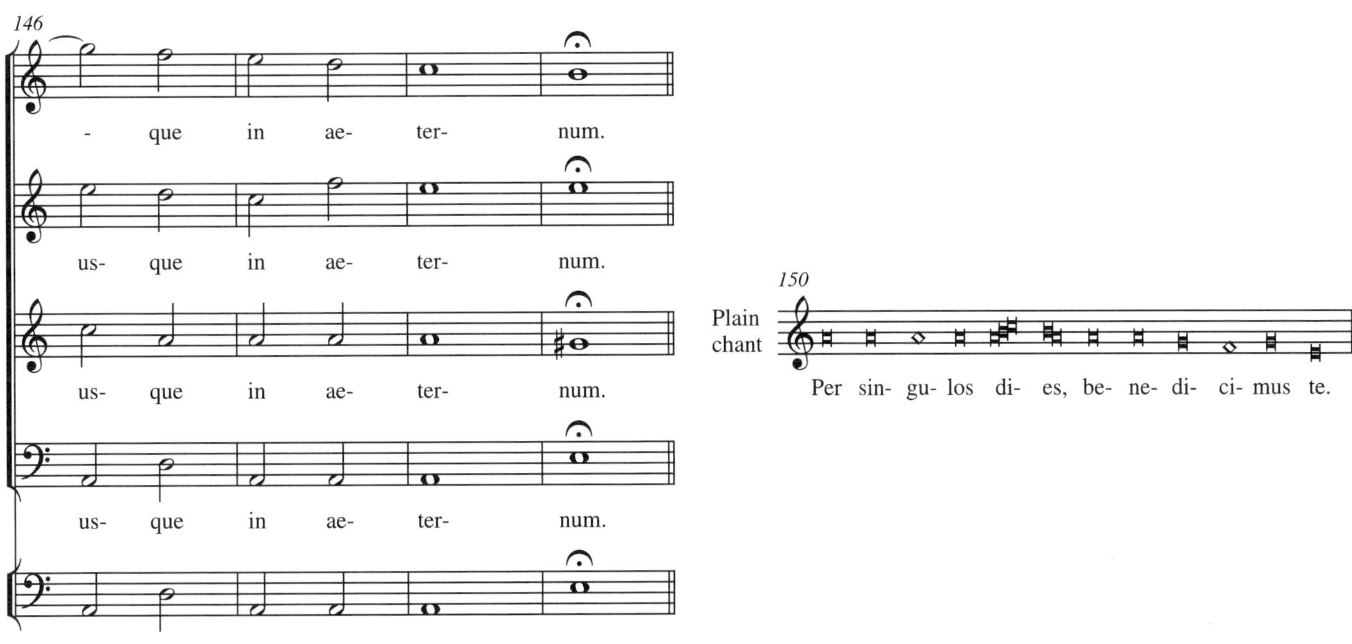
146
- que in ae- ter- num.
us- que in ae- ter- num.
us- que in ae- ter- num.
us- que in ae- ter- num.
150
Plain chant
Per sin- gu- los di- es, be- ne- di- ci- mus te.

151
[D1]
Et lau- da- mus no- men tu- um in sae- cu- lum, et in sae- cu- lum sae-
[D2]
Et lau- da- mus no- men tu- um in sae- cu- lum, et in sae- cu- lum sae-
[BD]
Et lau- da- mus no- men tu- um in sae- cu- lum, et in sae- cu- lum sae-
[B]
Et lau- da- mus no- men tu- um in sae- cu- lum et in sae- cu- lum sae-
Org.

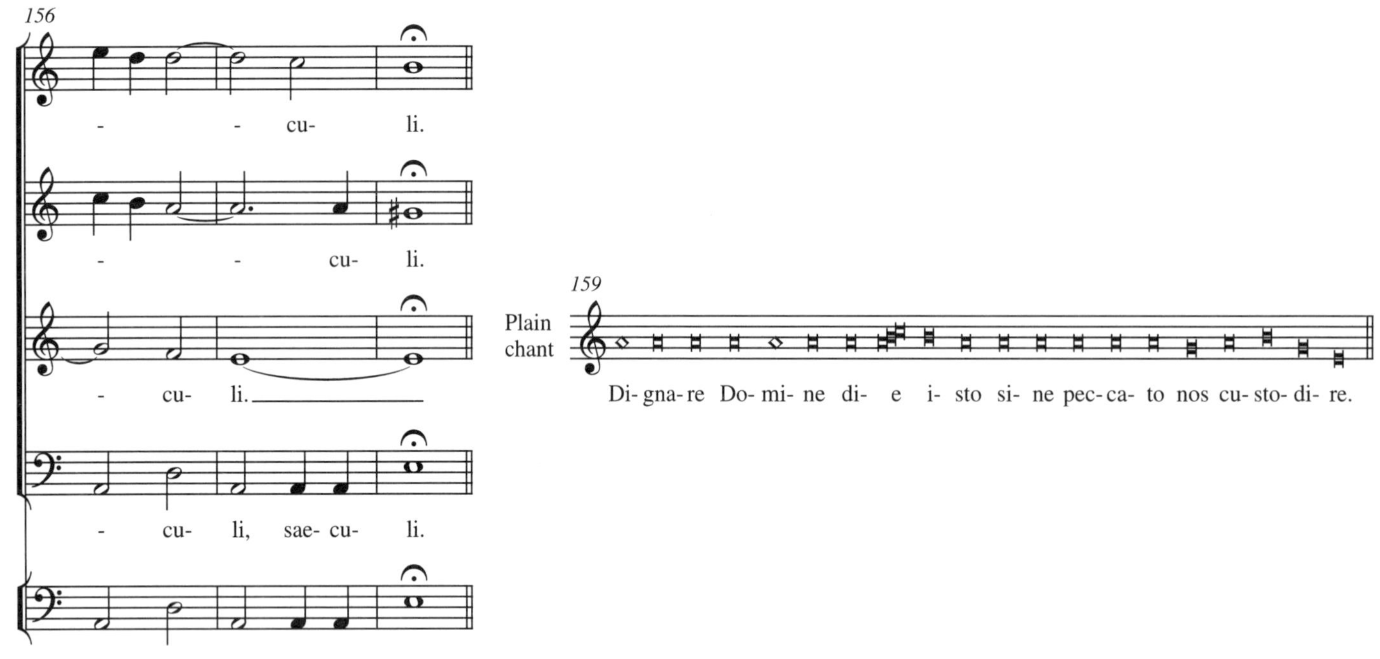
156
- - cu- li.
- - cu- li.
- cu- li.
- cu- li, saec- cu- li.
159
Plain chant
Di- gna- re Do- mi- ne di- e i- sto si- ne pec- ca- to nos cu- sto- di- re.

160
[BD]
Mi- se- re- re no- stri Do- - - - mi- ni,
Org.

166
[D1]
mi- se- re- - re, mi- se- re- - re no- stri.
[D2]
mi- se- - re- - - - re no- stri.
[BD]
mi- se- re- re no- - stri.
[B]
mi- se- re- re, mi- se- re- - re no- stri.
Org.

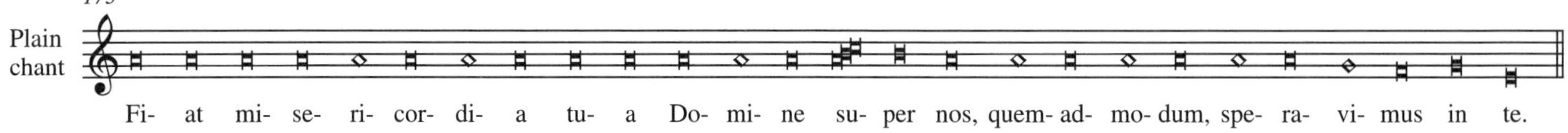
173
Plain chant
Fi- at mi- se- ri- cor- di- a tu- a Do- mi- ne su- per nos, quem- ad- mo- dum, spe- ra- vi- mus in te.

174
[D1]
In te Do- mi- ne spe- ra- vi: non con-
[D2]
In te Do- mi- ne spe- ra- vi: non con-
[BD]
In te Do- mi- ne spe- ra- vi: non con-
[B]
In te Do- mi- ne spe- ra- vi: non con-
Org.
176
-fun- dar in ae- ter- num, in ae- ter- num.
-fun- dar in ae- - ter- - num, in ae- ter- num.
-fun- dar in ae- ter- num.
-fun- dar in ae- ter- num, in ae- ter- num.

Psalms

9. Beatus vir

Psalm 111

16
-ra- ti- o, ge- ne- ra- ti- o, ge- ne- ra- - ti- o re- cto- rum be-
ge- ne- ra- ti- o, ge- ne- ra- ti- o re- cto- rum be- ne- di-
ge- ne- ra- ti- o re- cto- rum be- ne- di-
ge- ne- ra- ti- o re- cto- rum be- ne- di-
21
-ne- di- ce- tur. Glo- ri- a et di- vi- ti- ae in do- mo e-
-ce- tur.
-ce- tur.
-ce- tur.
26
-jus: et ju- sti- - ti- a e- jus ma- net in sae- cu- lum, in
et ju- sti- ti- a e- - jus ma- net in sae- cu- lum, in
et ju- sti- ti- a e- jus ma- net, ma- net in sae- cu- lum,
et ju- sti- ti- a e- jus ma- - net in sae- cu- lum,

31
sae- cu-lum sae- cu- li, in
sae- cu-lum sae- cu- li, in sae- - cu-lum sae- - cu- li,
in sae- cu-lum sae- cu- li, in
in sae- cu- lum sae- cu- li, in
36
sae- cu- lum sae- - cu- li, sae- cu- li.
in sae- cu- lum, in sae- cu- lum sae- cu- li.
sae- cu- lum, in sae- cu- lum, in sae- cu- lum sae- cu- li. Ex- or- tum est
sae- cu- lum, in sae- cu- lum, in sae- cu- lum sae- cu- li. Ex-
41
Ex- or- tum est in te- ne- bris lu- men, lu- men re- ctis:
mi- se- ri-
in te- ne- bris, in te- ne- bris lu- - men re- ctis:
-or- tum est in te- ne- bris lu- men re- ctis:

46
mi- se- ri- cors, et mi- se-
-cors, et mi- se- ra- tor, et ju- stus, et mi- se- ra- tor,
mi- se- ri- cors, et mi- se- ra-
mi- se- ri- cors, et mi- se-
51
-ra- tor, et ju- stus, et ju- stus. Ju- cun- dus ho-
et ju- stus, et ju- stus. Ju- cun- dus
- tor, et ju- stus, et ju- stus.
-ra- tor, et ju- stus, et ju- stus.
56
-mo qui mi- se- re- - tur et com- mo- dat, dis- po- net ser- mo- nes su-
ho- mo qui mi- se- re- tur et com- mo- dat, dis- po-
dis- po- net ser- mo- nes, ser- mo-
dis- po- net ser- mo- nes, ser- mo-

61
-os in ju- di- ci- o, in ju- di- ci- o: qui- - a in ae-
- net ser- mo- nes su- os in ju- di- ci- o:
- nes, ser- mo- nes su- os in ju- di- ci- o:
- nes su- os in ju- di- ci- o:
66
-ter- num non com- mo- ve- bi- tur, in ae- ter- num non
qui- a in ae- ter- num, in ae- ter-
qui- a in ae- ter- num non com-
qui- a in ae- ter- num non com- mo-
71
com- mo- ve- bi- tur.
-num non com- mo- ve- bi- tur. In me- mo- ri- a ae- ter- na e- rit ju-
-mo- ve- bi- tur.
-ve- bi- tur.

76
ab au- di- ti- o- ne ma- la non ti- me- bit, non ti- me-
-stus: ab au- di- ti- o- ne ma- la non ti- me- bit, non ti- me- bit, non ti- me-
ma- la non ti- me- bit, non ti- me- bit, non ti- me-
ab au- di- ti- o- ne ma- la non ti- me- bit, non ti- me-
81
-bit.
-bit.
-bit. Pa- ra- tum cor e- jus spe- ra- re in Do- mi-
-bit.
86
con- fir- ma- tum est cor e- jus, cor e- jus: non com- mo-
non com- mo-
-no, con- fir- ma- - tum est cor e- jus: non com- mo-
non com- mo-

91
-ve- bi- tur do- nec de- spi- ci- at i- ni- mi- - cos su- os.
-ve- bi- tur do- nec de- spi- ci- at i- ni- mi- - cos su- os. Di-
-ve- bi- tur do- nec de- spi- ci- at i- ni- mi- cos su- os.
-ve- bi- tur do- nec de- spi- ci- at i- ni- mi- cos su- os.
96
ju- sti- ti- a, ju- sti- ti- a, ju- sti- ti-
-sper- sit, de- dit pau- pe- ri- bus: ju- sti- ti- a, ju- sti- ti- a, ju-
ju- sti- ti- a, ju-
ju- sti- ti- a, ju- sti- ti- a
101
-a e- jus ma- - net in sae- cu- lum, in sae- cu- lum sae- cu- li:
-sti- ti- a e- jus ma- net in sae- cu- lum sae- cu- li:
-sti- ti- a e- jus ma- net in sae- cu- lum sae- cu- li:
e- jus ma- net in sae- cu- lum, in sae- cu- lum sae- cu- li:

106
cor- nu e- jus ex- al- ta- bi- tur in glo- ri- a, ex-
ex- - al- ta- bi-
ex- al- ta- bi- tur in glo- ri-
ex- al- ta- bi-
111
- al- ta- bi- tur in glo- ri- a. Pec- ca- tor vi- de- bit, vi-
-tur in glo- ri- a, in glo- ri- a. Pec- ca- tor vi-
-a, in glo- ri- a, in glo- ri- a.
-tur in glo- ri- a, in glo- ri- a.
116
-de- bit, et i- ra- sce- tur, den- ti- bus su- is fre- met et ta-
-de- bit, et i- ra- sce- - tur, den- ti- bus
et i- ra- sce- tur, den- - ti- bus su- is fre-
et i- ra- sce- tur, den- ti- bus su- is fre- met et ta-

121
-be- scet: de- si- de- ri- um pec- ca- to- rum per- i- bit,
et ta- ba- scet: de- si-
-met et ta- be- scet: de- si-
-be- scet: de- si-
126
de- si- de- ri- um pec- ca- to- rum per- i- bit.
-de- ri- um pec- ca- to- rum per- i- bit. Glo- ri- a
-de- ri- um pec- ca- to- rum per- i- bit.
-de- ri- um pec- ca- to- rum per- i- bit.
131
Sic- ut
Pa- tri, et Fi- li- o, et Spi- ri- tu- i San- cto.
Sic-
Sic- ut

136
e- rat in prin- ci- - pi- o, et nunc, et sem- per, et in sae- cu-
in prin- ci- pi- o, et nunc, et sem- per,
-ut e- rat in prin- ci- pi- o, et nunc, et sem- per,
e- rat in prin- ci- pi- o, et nunc, et sem- per,
141
-la sae- cu- lo- - rum, a- men, sae- cu- lo- rum. A men.
et in sae- cu- la sae- cu- lo- rum, a- men, sae- cu- lo- rum. A- men.
sae- cu- lo- rum. A- men.
sae- cu- lo- rum. A- men.

10. Dixit Dominus

Psalm 109

15
tu- o- rum. Vir- gam vir- tu- tis tu- ae e- mit tet Do- mi-
- dum tu- o- rum.
tu- o- rum.
- rum.
21
-nus ex Si- on: do- mi- na- re in me- di- o, do- mi- na-
do- mi- na- re, do- mi- na- re, do- mi- na- re in
do- mi- na- re, do- mi- na- re in me- di-
do- mi- na- re, do- mi- na- re in me- di-
26
-re in me- di- o, in me- di- o i- ni- mi- co- rum tu- o-
me- di- o, in me- di- o i- ni- mi- co- rum tu- o- rum, i- ni- mi- co- - rum tu- o-
-o i- ni- mi- co- rum tu- o- rum, i- ni- mi- co- - rum tu- o-
-o, in me- di- o i- ni- mi- co- rum tu- o-

31
-rum.
-rum.
-rum. Te- cum prin- ci- pi- um in di- e vir- tu- tis tu- ae
-rum.
37
ex u- te- ro an- te lu- ci- fe-
ex u- te- ro an- te lu- ci- fe-
in splen- do- ri- bus san- cto- rum: ex u- te- ro an- te lu- ci- fe-
ex u- te- ro an- te lu- ci- fe-
42
-rum, lu- ci- fe- rum ge- nu- i te. Ju- ra- vit Do- mi- nus, ju- ra- vit
-rum, lu- ci- fe- rum ge- nu- i te. Ju- ra- vit
-rum, lu- ci- fe- rum ge- nu- i te.
-rum, lu- ci- fe- rum ge- nu- i te.

47
Do- mi- nus, et non pae- ni- te- bit e- um: Tu es sa- cer- dos
Do- mi- nus, et non pae- ni- te- - bit e- um: Tu
Tu es sa- cer- dos, tu
Tu es sa- cer- dos, tu
52
in ae- ter- num se- cun- dum or- - di- nem, or- di-
es sa- cer- dos in ae- ter- num se- cun- dum or- di-nem, or- di-
es sa-cer- dos in ae- ter- num se- cun- dum or- - di- nem
es sa- cer- dos in ae- ter- num se- cun- dum or- - di- nem Mel-
57
-nem Mel- chi- se- dech. Do- mi- nus a de- xtris tu- is, con-
-nem Mel- chi- se- dech. Do- mi- nus a de- xtris tu- is,
Mel- chi- se- dech.
-chi- se- dech.

62
-fre- git in di- e i- rae su- ae re- ges, con- fre-
con- fre- git in di-
con- fre- git in di- e
con- fre- git in di- e i-
67
-git in di- e i- rae su- ae re- ges. Ju- di-
-e i- rae su- ae re- ges.
i- rae su- ae re- ges. Ju- di- ca- bit
- rae, i- rae su- - ae re- ges. Ju- di- ca-
72
-ca- bit in na- ti- o- ni- bus, im- ple- bit ru- i- nas: con- quas-
con- quas- sa- bit ca- pi-
in na- ti- o- ni- bus, im- ple- bit ru- i- nas: con- quas-
-bit in na- ti- o- ni- bus, im- ple- bit ru- i- nas: con- quas-

77
-sa- bit in ter- ra, in ter- ra mul- to- rum.
-ta in ter- - ra mul- to- rum, in ter- ra mul- to- rum.
-sa- bit ca- pi- ta in ter- ra, in ter- ra mul- to- rum. De tor-
-sa- bit ca- pi- ta in ter- ra mul- to- rum.
82
De tor- ren- - te in vi- a bi- bet, in vi- a
in vi- - a bi- bet,
-ren- te in vi- a, in vi- a bi- - bet, in vi- a bi-
in vi- a bi- bet, in
87
bi- bet: pro- pte- re-
bi- bet: pro- pte- re- a ex- al- ta- bit ca- put,
-bet, bi- bet: pro- pte- re-
vi- a bi- bet:

92
-a, pro- pte- re- a ex- al- ta- bit ca- put.
pro- pte- - re- a ex- al- ta- bit ca- put.
-a ex- al- ta- bit, ex- al- ta- bit ca- put.
pro- pte- re- a ex- al- ta- bit ca- put, ex- al- ta- bit ca- put.
97
Glo- ri- a Pa- tri, et Fi- li- o, et Fi- - li- o, et
Glo- - ri- a Pa- tri, et Fi- - li- o, et
et
et
102
Fi- li- o, et Spi- ri- tu- i San- cto, et Spi- ri-
Fi- li- o, et Spi- ri-
Fi- li- o, et Spi- ri-
Fi- li- o, et Spi- ri-

107
-tu- i San- cto. Sic- - ut e- rat in prin-ci- pi- o, et
-tu- i San- cto. Sic- ut e- - rat in prin- ci- pi- o, et
- tu- i San- cto.
-tu- i San- cto.
113
nunc, et sem- per, et in sae-cu- la sae- - cu- lo- - rum. A- men.
nunc, et sem- per, et in sae- cu- la sae-cu- lo- rum. A- men.
et in sae-cu- la sae- cu- lo- rum. A- men, a- men.
et in sae-cu- la sae- cu- lo- - rum. A- men.

11. Ecce quam bonum

Psalm 132

16
-ron. Ec- ce quam bo- num et quam ju- cun- dum, ha- bi- ta- re fra- tres
-ron. ha- bi- ta- re fra- tres, ha- bi- ta- re fra-
-ron.
-ron.
22
in u- num. Quod de- scen- dit in o- - ram ve- sti- men- ti
- tres in u- num. Quod de- scen- dit in o- ram ve- - sti- men- ti
Quod de- scen- dit in o- ram ve- sti- men- ti
Quod de- scen- dit in o- ram ve- sti- men- ti
27
e- jus: sic- ut ros Her- mon, qui de- scen- dit in mon-
e- jus: sic- ut ros Her- mon, qui de- scen- dit in mon-
e- jus: sic- ut ros Her- mon, qui de- scen- dit in mon- tem
e- jus: sic- ut ros Her- mon, qui de- scen- dit in mon-

32
-tem Si- on. Ec- ce quam bo- num et quam ju- cun- dum,
-tem Si- on. ha- bi- ta- re
Si- on.
-tem Si- on.
38
ha- bi- ta- re fra- tres in u- - num. Quo- ni-
fra- tres, ha- bi- ta- re fra- tres in u- num. Quo- ni- am il- lic man- da-
Quo- ni- am il- lic
Quo- ni- am il- lic man-
43
-am il- lic man- da- vit Do- mi- nus be- ne- di- cti- o- nem, et
- vit, man- da- vit Do- mi- nus be- ne- di- cti- o- nem,
man- da- vit Do- mi- nus be- ne- di- cti- o- nem,
-da- vit, man- da- vit Do- mi- nus be- ne- di- cti- o- nem,

48
vi- tam us- que in sae- - cu- lum, us- que in sae- cu- lum. Ec- ce quam
et vi- tam us- - que in sae- cu- lum.
et vi- tam us- que in sae- - cu- lum.
et vi- tam, et vi- tam us- que in sae- cu- lum.
54
bo- num et quam ju- cun- dum, ha- bi- ta- re fra- tres in u- - num.
ha- bi- ta- re fra- tres, ha- bi- ta- re fra- tres in u- num.
60
Glo- ri- a Pa- tri, et Fi- li- o, et Spi- ri- tu- i San-
Glo- ri- a Pa- tri, et Fi- li- o, et Spi- ri- tu- i San-
Glo- ri- a Pa- tri, et Fi- - li- o, et Spi- ri- tu- i San-
Glo- ri- a Pa- tri, et Fi- li- o, et Spi- ri- tu- i San-

66
-cto. Sic- ut e- rat in prin- ci- pi- o, et nunc, et sem- per, et in
-cto. et nunc, et sem- per, et in
-cto. et in
-cto. et in
71
sae- cu- la sae- - cu- lo- rum, a- men, et in sae- cu- la, et in sae- cu- la sae- cu-
sae- cu- la sae- cu- lo- rum, a- men, et in sae- cu- la, et in sae- cu- la sae- cu- lo-
sae- cu- la sae- cu- lo- rum, a- men, et in sae- cu- la sae- cu- lo-
sae- cu- la sae- cu- lo- rum, a- men, et in sae- cu- la sae- cu- lo-
76
-lo- rum. A- men, a- - men.
- rum. A- men, a- - - - men.
- rum. A- men, a- - - men.
- rum. A- men, a- - - men.

12. Laetatus sum

Psalm 121

16
[D1]
-ru- sa- lem, quae ae- di- fi- ca- tur, ae- di- fi- ca- tur ut ci- vi- tas:
[D2]
Je- ru- sa- lem, quae ae- di- fi- ca- tur ut ci- vi- tas:
[B.c.]
21
cu- jus par- ti- ci- pa- - ti- o e- jus in id- i-
cu- jus par- ti- ci- pa- ti- o e- jus in id- i-
26
[D1]
-psum. Il- luc e- nim a- scen- de- runt tri- bus, tri- bus Do- mi- ni: te- sti-
[D2]
-psum. Il- luc e- nim a- scen- de- runt tri- bus, tri- bus Do- mi- ni: te- sti-
[HC]
Il- luc e- nim a- scen- de- runt tri- bus, tri- bus Do- mi- ni: te- sti-
[B]
Il- luc e- nim a- scen- de- runt tri- bus, tri- bus Do- mi- ni: te- sti-
[B.c.]
32
-mo- ni- um Is- ra- el ad con- fi- ten- dum no- mi- ni Do- mi- ni.
-mo- ni- um Is- ra- el ad con- fi- ten- dum no- mi- ni Do- mi- ni.
-mo- ni- um Is- ra- el ad con- fi- ten- dum no- mi- ni Do- mi- ni.
-mo- ni- um Is- ra- el ad con- fi- ten- dum no- mi- ni Do- mi- ni.

37
[D1]
[B.c.]
Qui- a il- lic se- de- runt se- des in ju- di- ci- o, se- des
42
[D1]
[D2]
[HC]
[B]
[B.c.]
su- per domum Da- vid. Ro- ga- te quae ad pa- cem sunt Je-
se- des su- per do- mum Da- vid. Ro- ga- te quae ad pa- cem sunt Je-
Ro- ga- te quae ad pa- cem sunt Je-
Ro- ga- te quae ad pa- cem sunt Je-
47
-ru- sa- lem: et a- bun- dan- ti- a di- - li- gen- ti- bus te. Fi- at
-ru- sa- lem: et a- bun- dan- ti- a di- - li- gen- ti- bus te.
-ru- sa- lem: et a- bun- dan- ti- a di- li- gen- ti- bus te.
-ru- sa- lem: et a- bun- dan- ti- a di- li- gen- ti- bus te.
52
[D1]
[D2]
[B.c.]
pax in vir- tu- te tu- a: et a- bun- dan- ti- a in tur- ri- bus tu-
et a- bun-dan- ti- a in tur- ri- bus tu-

57
[D1]
[D2]
[HC]
[B]
[B.c.]
-is. Propter fratres me- os et pro- xi- mos me- os, lo-
-is. Propter fra- tres me- os et pro- xi- mos me- os, lo-
Propter fra- tres me- os et pro- xi- mos me- os, lo-
Propter fra- tres me- os et pro- xi- mos me- os, lo-
62
-que- bar pa- - cem de te: Pro- pter do- mum Do- mi- ni
-que- bar pa- - cem de te:
-que- bar pa- - cem de te:
-que- bar pa- - cem de te:
67
De- i no- stri, quae- si- vi bo- na, bo- na ti- bi. Glo-
quae- si- vi bo- na, bo- na ti- bi.
quae- si- vi bo- na ti- bi.
quae- si- vi bo- na, bo- na ti- bi.

73
-ri- a Pa- tri, et Fi- li- o, et Spi- ri- tu- i San-
et Spi- ri- tu- i San-
78
-cto. Sic- ut e- rat in prin- ci- pi- o, et nunc, et sem- per,
-cto. Sic- ut e- rat in prin- ci- pi- o, et nunc, et sem- per,
Sic- ut e- rat in prin- ci- pi- o, et nunc, et sem- per,
Sic- ut e- rat in prin- ci- pi- o, et nunc, et sem- per,
83
et in sae- cu- la sae- cu- lo- rum. A- men.
et in sae- cu- la sae- cu- lo- rum. A- men, a- men.
sae- cu- lo- rum. A- men, a- men.
sae- cu- lo- rum. A- men.

13. Laudate pueri (1)

Psalm 112

17
[D1]
-tu us- que ad oc- ca- sum, lau- da- bi- le no- - men Do- mi- ni, no- men
[D2]
or- tu us- que ad oc- ca- sum, lau- da- bi- le no- men
[B.c.]
23
[D1]
Do- mi- ni, no- men Do- mi- ni. Ex- cel- sus su- per om- nes
[D2]
Do- mi- ni, no- - men Do- mi- ni. Ex- cel- sus su- per om- nes
[HC]
Ex- cel- sus su- per om- nes
[B]
Ex- cel- sus su- per om- nes
[B.c.]
28
gen- tes Do- mi- nus, et su- per cae- los glo- ri- a e- jus. Quis
gen- tes Do- mi- nus, et su- per cae- los glo- ri- a, glo- ri- a e- jus.
gen- tes Do- mi- nus, et su- per cae- los glo- ri- a e- jus.
gen- tes Do- mi- nus, et su- per cae- los glo- ri- a e- jus.
34
[D1]
sic- ut Do- mi- nus De- us no- ster, qui in al- tis ha- bi- tat, et hu-
[B.c.]

40
[D1]
-mi- li- a re- spi- cit in cae- lo et in ter- ra? Su- sci- tans a ter- ra in- o-
[D2]
Su- sci- tans a ter- ra in- o-
[HC]
Su- sci- tans a ter- ra in- o-
[B]
Su- sci- tans a ter- ra in- o-
[B.c.]
46
-pem, et de ster- co- re e- ri- gens pau- pe- rem:
-pem, et de ster- co- re e- - ri- gens pau- pe- rem: Ut col- lo- cet
-pem, et de ster- co- re e- ri- gens pau- pe- rem:
-pem, et de ster- co- re e- ri- gens pau- pe- rem:
51
[D2]
e- um cum prin- ci- pi- bus, cum prin- ci- pi- bus po-
[B.c.]
56
[D1]
Qui ha- bi- ta- - re fa- cit ste- ri- lem in
[D2]
- pu- li su- i. Qui ha- bi- ta- - re fa- cit ste- ri- lem in
[HC]
Qui ha- bi- ta- - re fa- cit ste- ri- lem in
[B]
Qui ha- bi- ta- - re fa- cit ste- ri- lem in
[B.c.]

61
do- mo, ma- trem fi- li- o- rum lae- tan- tem. Glo-
do- mo, ma- trem fi- li- o- rum lae- tan- tem.
do- mo, ma- trem fi- li- o- rum lae- tan- tem.
do- mo, ma- trem fi- li- o- rum lae- tan- tem.
66
- ri- a Pa- tri, et Fi- li- o, et Spi- ri- - tu- i
71
San- cto. Sic- ut e- rat in prin- ci- pi- o, et nunc, et sem-
Sic- ut e- rat in prin- ci- pi- o, et nunc, et sem-
Sic- ut e- rat in prin- ci- pi- o, et nunc, et sem-
Sic- ut e- rat in prin- ci- pi- o, et nunc, et sem-

76
-per, et in sae- cu- la sae- cu- lo- rum, a- men, et in sae- cu-
-per, et in sae- cu-
-per, et in sae-
-per, et in sae- cu-
80
-la sae- cu- lo- rum, a- men, sae- cu- lo- rum. A- men.
-la sae- cu- lo- rum, a- men, sae- cu- lo- rum. A- men.
- cu- la sae- cu- lo- rum, a- men, sae- cu- lo- rum. A- men.
-la sae- cu- lo- rum, a- men, sae- cu- lo- rum. A- men.

14. Laudate pueri (2)

Psalm 112

19
[D]
us- que ad oc- ca- sum, lau- da- bi- le no- men Do- mi-
[HT]
lau- da- bi- le no- men Do- mi-
Org.
25
-ni, lau- da- bi- le no- men Do- mi- ni.
-ni, lau- da- bi- le no- men Do- mi-
31
[D]
Ex- cel- sus su- per om- nes gen- tes Do- mi- nus,
[HC]
Ex- cel- sus su- per om- nes gen- tes Do- mi- nus,
[HT]
-ni. Ex- cel- sus su- per om- nes gen- tes Do- mi- nus,
[B]
Ex- cel- sus su- per om- nes gen- tes Do- mi- nus,
Org.
37
et su- per cae- los glo- ri- a e- jus. Quis sic- ut
et su- per cae- los glo- ri- a e- jus.
et su- per cae- los glo- ri- a e- jus.
et su- per cae- los glo- ri- a e- jus.

43
[D]
Org.
Do- mi- nus De- us no- ster, qui in al- tis ha- bi- tat, et hu-
49
-mi- li- a re- - spi- cit in cae- lo et in ter- ra?
55
[D]
Su- sci- tans a ter- ra in- o- pem, et de ster- co- re e- ri- gens, e- ri- gens
[HC]
Su- sci- tans a ter- ra in- o- pem, et de ster- co- re e- ri- gens
[HT]
Su- sci- tans a ter- ra in- o- pem, et de ster- co- re e- ri- gens, e- ri-
[B]
Su- sci- tans a ter- ra in- o- pem, et de ster- co- re e- ri- gens
Org.
60
pau- pe- rem: Ut col- lo- cet e- um
pau- pe- rem:
-gens pau- pe- rem: Ut col- lo- cet e- um cum prin-
pau- pe- rem:

66
[D]
cum prin- ci- pi- bus po- pu- li su- i,
[HT]
-ci- pi- bus po- pu- li su- i,
Org.
72
cum prin- ci- pi- bus po- pu- li su- i, cum prin- ci- pi- bus
cum prin- ci- pi- bus po- pu- li su- i, cum prin- ci- pi- bus
78
[D]
po- pu- li su- i. Qui ha- bi- ta- re fa- cit ste- ri- lem in do-
[HC]
Qui ha- bi- ta- re fa- cit ste- ri- lem, ste- ri- lem in do-
[HT]
po- pu- li su- i. Qui ha- bi- ta- re fa- cit ste- ri- lem in do-
[B]
Qui ha- bi- ta- re fa- cit ste- ri- lem in do-
Org.
84
-mo, ma- trem fi- li- o- rum lae- tan- tem, fi- li- o- rum lae- tan-
-mo,
-mo,
-mo,

89
-tem, ma- trem fi- li- o- rum lae- tan- tem, ma- trem fi- li- o-
ma- - trem fi- li- o- rum lae- tan- tem, ma- - trem fi- li-
ma- trem fi- li- o- rum lae- tan- tem, ma- trem fi- li-
ma- trem fi- li- o- rum lae- tan- tem, ma- trem fi- li-
94
- rum lae- tan- tem. Glo- - ri- a Pa- tri,
-o- rum lae- tan- tem.
-o- rum lae- tan- tem. et Fi-
-o- rum lae- tan- tem.
102
et Spi- ri- tu- i San- cto. Sic- ut e- rat
Sic- ut e- - rat
- - li- o, Sic- ut e- rat
Sic- ut e- rat

110
in prin- ci- pi- o, et nunc,_ et sem- per, et in sae- cu- la sae- cu-
in prin- ci- pi- o, et nunc, et sem- per,
in prin- ci- pi- o, et nunc, et sem- per,
in prin- ci- pi- o, et nunc, et sem- per,
115
-lo- rum, a- men, et in sae- cu- la sae- cu- lo- rum, sae- cu- lo- rum, a-
120
-men, sae- cu- lo- rum, a- men, sae- cu- lo- rum. A- - men.
sae- cu- lo- rum, sae- cu- lo- - rum. A- men.
sae- cu- lo- rum,_ a- - men, sae- - cu- lo- rum. A- men.
sae- cu- lo- rum._ A- men, a- - - men.

Independent Mass Movements

15. Kyrie

[Dessus 1]
[Dessus 2]
[Bas-dessus]
[Basse]
[Basse continue]
Ky- ri- e e- le- i- son, e- le- - i-
Ky- - ri- e e- le- -
Ky- ri-
6
-son, e- le- i- son, e- - le- i- son. Chri-
- i- son, e- le- - i- son. Chri- ste e- le-
Ky- - ri- e e- lei- son.
-e e- le- i- son, e- le- i- son. Chri- - ste
12
- ste e- le- i- son, e- le- i- son, e- le- - i- son.
- - i- son, Chri- - ste e- - le- - i- son.
e- le- - i- son, Chri- - ste e- le- - i- son.

17
Ky- ri- e e- le- i- son, Ky- ri- e e- le- i- son,
Ky- - ri- e
Ky- ri- e e- le- i- son,
Ky- ri- e e- le- i- son,
22
e- le- - - i- son, e- le- - i- son.
e- le- - i- son, e- le- i- son, e- le- - i- son.
e- le- - i- son, e- le- - i- son.
e- le- - - i- son, e- le- - i- son.

16. Sanctus, Benedictus

15
ter- ra glo- ri- a tu- a, glo- - ri- a tu- a. Ho-
- ra glo- ri- a tu- a. Ho- san-
ter- ra glo- ri- a tu- - a.
- ra, glo- - ri- a tu- a, glo- ri- a tu- a.
21
-san- na in ex- cel- - sis, ho- san- -
- na, ho- - san- - na, ho-
ho- san- na in ex-
Ho- san- na in ex- cel- sis, ho- san- na, ho- san-
26
- na in ex- cel- sis. qui
-san- na, ho- san- - na in ex- cel- sis. Be- ne- di- ctus qui
-cel- sis, ho- san- na in ex- cel- sis.
- na, ho- san- na in ex- cel- sis. qui
Fine

32
ve- nit in no- mi- ne Do- - - mi- ni.
ve- nit, qui ve- nit in no- mi- ne Do- - mi- ni.
qui ve- nit in no- mi- ne Do- - mi- ni.
ve- nit in no- mi- ne Do- - mi- ni.
D.S. al Fine

17. Agnus Dei

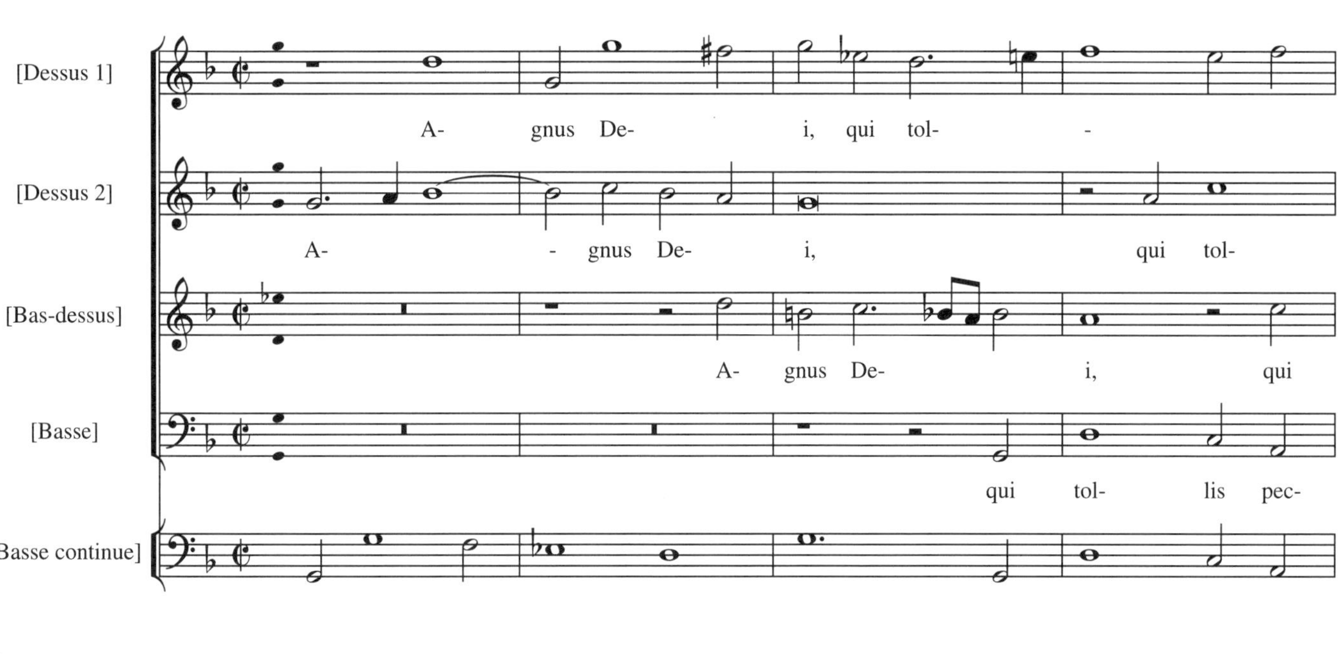
[Dessus 1]
A- gnus De- i, qui tol- -
[Dessus 2]
A- - gnus De- i, qui tol-
[Bas-dessus]
A- gnus De- i, qui
[Basse]
qui tol- lis pec-
[Basse continue]

5
-lis pec- ca- ta mun- di: do- na
-lis pec- ca- ta mun- di: do- - na e- is,
tol- lis pec- ca- ta mun- di: do- na e-
-ca- ta mun- di:

10
e- is, do- na e- - is re- qui- em.
do- na e- - is, do- na e- is re- qui- em.
- is, do- na e- - is re- qui- em.
do- na e- is, do- na e- is re- qui- em.
16
Plain chant
A- gnus De- i, qui tol- lis pec- ca- ta mun- di: do- na e- is re- qui- em.
17
[D1]
A-
[D2]
A-
[BD]
[B]
[B.c.]
18
-gnus De- i, qui tol- - lis pec- ca- ta mun-
- gnus De- i, qui tol- lis pec- ca- ta mun-
A- gnus De- i, qui tol- lis pec- ca- ta mun-
qui tol- lis pec- ca- ta mun-

23
-di: do- na e- is, do- na e-
-di: do- - na e- is, do- na e- - is, do- na
-di: do- na e- - is, do- na e-
-di: do- na e- is, do- na
29
- is re- qui- em sem- - pi- ter- nam.
e- is re- qui- em sem- - pi- ter- - nam.
- is re- qui- em sem- - pi- ter- nam.
e- is re- qui- em sem- - pi- ter- nam.

18. Libera me

[Dessus 1]
[Dessus 2]
[Bas-dessus]
[Basse]
[Basse continue]
de mor- - te, de mor- te ae-
de mor- - te ae-
Li- be- ra me, Do- mi- ne, de mor- te ae- ter-
de mor- te, de mor- te
6
-ter- na, in di- e il- la tre- men- -
-ter- na, in di- e il- la,
- na, in di- e
ae- ter- na, in di- e il- - la tre- men- da,
11
-da, in di- - e il- la tre- men- - da: Quan- do cae-
in di- e il- la tre- men- da:
il- la tre- men- da, tre- men- - da:
in di- e il- la tre- men- - da: Quan- do

16
- - li, cae- li mo- ven- - di sunt
Quan- do cae- - li mo- ven- di sunt
Quan- do cae- - - li mo- ven- - di
cae- li, quan- do cae- li mo- ven- di sunt et
21
et ter- ra: Dum ve- - ne- ris, dum ve-
et ter- ra: Dum ve- - - ne- ris, dum ve-
sunt et ter- ra:
ter- ra: Dum
27
- ne- ris ju- - di- ca- re, ju- di- ca- re, ju- di- ca- re sae- cu-
- ne- ris ju- di- ca- re sae- cu- lum per i- gnem,
Dum ve- ne- ris ju- di- ca- - re sae-
ve- ne- ris ju- di- ca- re sae- cu- lum, sae- cu-

32
-lum, sae- cu- lum per i- gnem. Tre- mens fa- ctus sum e- go, et
sae- cu- lum per i- gnem. Tre- mens fa- ctus sum e- - go,
- cu- lum per i- gnem. Tre- mens fa- ctus sum e- go, et
-lum per i- gnem.
38
ti- me- o, et ti- me- o, dum di- scus- - si- o ve-
et ti- me- o, et ti- me- o, dum di- scus- si- o, di- scus- si- o
ti- me- o, et ti- me- o, dum di- scus- - si- o
43
- ne- rit, at- que ven- tu- - ra i- ra.
ve- ne- rit, at- que ven- tu- ra i- ra, i- ra.
ve- ne- rit, at- que ven- tu- - ra i- ra.

48
Di- es il- la, di- es i- rae, di- es i- rae, di- es i- rae,
Di- es il- la,
Di- es il- - la, di- es i- rae, di- es i- rae, di- es, di-
Di- es il- la, di- es, di- es i- rae,
54
di- es i- rae, di- es i- rae
di- es i- rae, di- - es i- rae,
-es i- rae, di- - es i- rae, ca- la- mi- ta-
di- es i- rae, ca-
59
ca- la- mi- ta- tis et mi- se- ri- ae,
ca- la- mi- ta-
-tis et mi- se- - ri- ae, ca- la- mi- ta- tis et mi- se- ri-
-la- mi- ta- tis et mi- se- ri- ae, ca- la- mi- ta- tis et

64
di- es ma- - gna, di- es ma- gna, di- es ma-
-tis et mi- se- ri- ae, di-
-ae, di- es ma- gna, di- - es ma- gna,
mi- se- ri- ae, di- es ma-
69
-gna, ma- gna et a- ma- - ra val- de.
- es ma- - gna et a- ma- - ra val- de.
di- es ma- gna et a- ma- ra val- de.
- - gna et a- ma- - ra val- de.
74
do- - na e- -
do- na e- -
Re- qui- em ae- ter- nam do- - na e- - is Do-
do- - na e- - is

79
- is Do- mi- ne: et lux, et lux per- pe- tu- a, et lux per- pe-
- is Do- mi- ne: et lux per- pe- tu- a, et lux, et lux, et
- mi- ne: et lux per- pe- - tu- a, et
Do- mi- ne: et lux per- pe-
84
- tu- a lu- - ce- at e- - is.
lux per- pe- - tu- a lu- ce- at, lu- ce- at e- is.
lux per- pe- tu- a lu- - ce- at, lu- ce- at e- is.
- tu- a lu- - ce- at e- - is.

19. Pie Jesu

[Dessus 1]
[Dessus 2]
[Haute-contre]
[Basse]
[Orgue]
Pi- - e Je- su Do- - mi-
Pi- - e
Pi- - e Je- su Do- - mi- ne,
Pi- - e Je- su,
8
-ne, Do- - - - mi- ne, do-
Je- su, pi- - e Je- su Do- mi-
Do- - mi- ne, Do- - - mi-
pi- - e Je- su Do- mi-
15
- - na e- is re- - qui- em,
-ne, do- - na e- - is re- qui- em,
-ne, do- na e- - is re- - qui- em,
-ne, do- na e- - is, do-

22
do- na e- is, do- na e- is re-
do- na e- is re-
do- na e- is, do- na e- is
- na e- is, do- na e- is re- qui-
29
- qui- em, do- na e- - - is re-
- qui- em, do- na e- - - - is
re- qui- em, do- na e- - is re-
-em, do- na e- - is
36
- qui- em. A- men.
re- qui- em. A- - men.
- qui- em. A- - - - men.
re- qui- em. A- - - men.

Complete Masses

Messe à 5 du 3e transposé

Kyrie

11
-son. Chri- ste e- le- i- son, Chri- ste e- le- i- son,
-son. Chri- ste e- le- i- son, Chri-
-son. Chri- ste e- le- i- son, Chri- ste e- le- i- son, Chri-
-son. Chri- ste e- le- i- son, Chri-
-son. Chri- ste e- le- i- son, Chri-
17
Chri- ste e- le- i- son, e- le- i- son.
-ste, Chri- ste e- le- i- son.
-ste, Chri- ste_ e- le- i- son. Ky- ri- e e-
-ste, Chri- ste e- le- i- son. Ky- ri- e e- le- i-
-ste, Chri- ste e- le- i- son. Ky- ri- e e-

23
Ky- ri- e, Ky- ri- e e- le- i- son,
Ky- ri- e e- le- i- son, Ky- ri- e, Ky- ri- e e- le- i- son,
-le- - i- son, Ky- ri- e, Ky- ri-
-son, e- le- i- son, Ky- ri- e, Ky- ri-
-le- - i- son, Ky- ri- e, Ky- ri-
28
Ky- ri- e e- le- i- son, Ky- ri- e e- le- i- son.
Ky- ri- e e- le- i- son, e- le- - i- son.
-e e- le- i- son, Ky- ri- e e- le- i- son, Ky- ri- e e- le- i- son.
-e e- le- i- son, Ky- ri- e, Ky- ri- e e- le- i- son, e- le- i- son.
-e e- le- i- son, Ky- ri- e e- le- i- son, e- le- i- son.

Gloria

Glo- ri- a in excel- sis De- o.

[Dessus 1]
[Dessus 2]
[Dessus 3]
[Bas-dessus]
[Basse]
Basse continue
Et in ter- ra pax ho- mi- ni- bus bo- nae vo- lun- ta-

5
-tis. Be- ne- di- ci- mus te.
Lau- da- mus te. Ad- - o- ra-
Lau- da- mus te. Ad- o- ra- -
Lau- da- mus te. Ad- o- ra-
Lau- da- mus te. Ad- o- ra- mus, ad- o-

10
Glo- ri- fi- ca- - mus te.
- mus te. Gra- ti- as a- gi- mus ti- bi
- mus te. Gra- ti- as a- gi- mus ti- - bi
- mus te. Gra- ti- as a- gi- mus ti- bi
-ra- mus te. Gra- ti- as a- gi- mus ti- bi
15
Do- mi- ne De- us,
pro- pter ma- - gnam glo- ri- am tu- am.
pro- pter ma- gnam glo- - ri- am tu- am.
pro- - pter ma- gnam glo- ri- am tu- am.
pro- pter ma- gnam glo- ri- am tu- am.

20
Rex cae- le- stis, De- us Pa- ter om- ni- po- tens.
Do- mi- ne Fi-
Do- mi- ne Fi-
Do- mi- ne Fi-
Do- mi- ne Fi-
25
3
-li u- ni- ge- ni- te Je- su Chri- ste.
-li u- ni- ge- ni- te Je- su Chri- ste.
-li u- ni- ge- ni- te Je- su Chri- ste. Do- mi- ne
-li u- ni- ge- ni- te Je- su Chri- ste.

31
3
Fi- - li- us
Fi- - li- us
Fi- - li- us
De- us, A- gnus De- i, A- gnus De- i, Fi- - li- us
Fi- - li- us
36
Pa- tris. Qui tol- -
Pa- tris. Qui tol- lis, qui
Pa- tris. Qui tol- lis, qui tol-
Pa- - tris. Qui tol- - lis,
Pa- tris. Qui tol- lis, qui

43
-lis pec- ca- - ta mun- - di,
tol- lis pec- ca- - ta mun- - di,
- lis pec- ca- - ta mun- di,
qui tol- lis pec- ca- - ta mun- di,
tol- lis pec- ca- - ta mun- di,
50
mi- - se- re- - re
mi- - se- re- re no-
mi- - se- re- - re no- bis,

57
no- bis, mi- se- re- - - re no- bis,
mi- - se-
mi- se- re- - re no- bis, mi- se- re- re,
- bis, mi- se- re- re no- -
mi- se- re- re no- bis,
64
mi- se- re- re no- - bis, mi- se- - re-
-re- re no- bis, mi- - se-
mi- - se- re- re,
- bis, mi- se- re- re no- bis,
mi- se- re- - re no- bis, mi- - se-

71
- re no- - bis. Qui tol- lis pec- ca- ta mun-
-re- re nobis.
mi- se- re- re no- - bis. Qui tol- lis, qui tol- lis pec- ca- ta mun-
mi- se- re- re no- bis.
-re- re no- - bis.
78
-di,
sus- ci- pe de- pre- ca- ti- o- - nem no- stram. Qui
-di, sus- ci- pe de- pre- ca- ti- o- nem no- stram.
sus- ci- pe de- pre- ca- ti- o- nem no- stram.
sus- ci- pe de- pre- ca- ti- o- - nem no- stram.

83
Qui se- des ad de- xte- ram Pa- tris, ad de- xte-
se- des ad de- xte- ram, qui se- - des ad de- xte- ram Pa- tris, ad
Qui se- des ad
88
- ram Pa- tris, mi- - se- re- re no- bis.
de- xte- ram Pa- tris, mi- - se- re- re no- bis.
mi- - se- re- re no- bis.
mi- se- re- re no- bis.
de- xte- ram Pa- tris, mi- - se- re- re no- bis.

94
Quo- ni- am tu so- lus san- ctus. Tu so- lus Do- - mi- nus, Tu
Quo- ni- am tu so- lus san- ctus. Tu so- lus Do- mi- nus.
Tu so- lus Do- mi- nus.
Tu so- lus Do- mi- nus.
99
so- lus Do- mi- nus. Tu so- - lus Al- tis- si- mus, Je-
Tu so- lus Al- tis- si- mus, Je- - su
Tu so- lus Al- tis- si- mus, Je- - su
Tu so- lus Al- tis- si- mus, Je- - su,
Tu so- lus Al- tis- si- mus, Je- - su

104
- su Chri- ste. Cum San- cto Spi- ri- tu, cum San-cto Spi- ri- tu,
Chri- - ste. Cum San- cto Spi- ri- tu,
Chri- - ste. Cum San- cto Spi- ri- tu,
Je- su Chri- ste. Cum San- cto Spi- ri- tu, in
Chri- - ste. Cum San- cto Spi- ri- tu,
110
in glo- ri- a De- i Pa- tris. A- men.
in glo- ri- a, in glo- ri- a De- - i Pa- tris. A- men.
in glo- ri- a De- i, De- i Pa- tris. A- men.
glo- ri- a De- - i, De- i Pa- tris. A- men.
in glo- ri- a, in glo- ri- a De- i Pa- tris. A- men.

Credo

Cre- do in u- num De- um.

[Dessus 1]
Pa- trem om- ni- po- ten- tem,
[Dessus 2]
fa- cto- rem cae- li, cae- li et ter-
[Dessus 3]
fa- cto- rem cae- li, cae- li et ter-
[Bas-dessus]
fa- cto- rem cae- li et ter-
[Basse]
fa- cto- rem cae- li et ter-
Basse continue

6
vi- si- bi- li- um om- ni- um, et in- vi- si- bi- li- um.
-rae, Et in u- num Do- mi-
-rae, Et in u- num Do- mi-
-rae, Et in u- num Do- mi-
-rae, Et in u- num Do- mi-

11
Et ex Pa- tre na- tum
-num Je- sum Chri- stum, Fi- li- um De- i u- ni- ge- ni- tum.
-num Je- sum Chri- stum, Fi- li- um De- i u- ni- ge- ni- tum.
-num Je- sum Chri- stum, Fi- li- um De- i u- ni-ge- ni- tum.
-num Je- sum Chri- stum, Fi- li- um De- i u- ni- ge- ni- tum.
17
an- te om- ni- a sae- cu- la.
De- um de De- o, lu- - men, lu- men de lu- mi- ne,
De- um de De- o, lu- men de lu- mi- ne,
De- um de De- o, lu- men, lu- men de lu- mi- ne,
De- um de De- o, lu- men, lu- men de lu- mi- ne,

23
Ge- - ni- tum, non fa- ctum, con- sub- stan- ti-
De- um ve- rum de De- o ve- ro.
De- um ve- rum de De- o, De- o ve- ro.
De- um ve- rum de De- o ve- ro.
De- um ve- rum de De- o ve- ro.
29
-a- lem Pa- tri: per quem om- ni- a fa- cta sunt.
Qui pro- pter nos ho- mi- nes, et
Qui pro- pter nos ho- mi- nes, et
Qui pro- pter nos ho- mi- nes,
Qui pro- pter nos ho- mi- nes, et

35
pro- pter no- stram sa- lu- tem de- scen- - dit,
pro- pter no- stram sa- lu- tem de- scen- dit de cae- lis, de
et pro- pter no- stram sa- lu- tem de- scen- dit de cae-
pro- pter no- stram sa- lu- tem de- scen- dit, de- scen-
40
Et in- car- na-
de- scen- dit de cae- lis. Et in- car- na-
cae- lis, de cae- lis. Et in- car- na-
-lis, de- scen- dit de cae- lis. Et in- car- na-
-dit de cae- lis, de cae- lis. Et in- car- na-

46
-tus est de Spi- ri- tu San- cto ex Ma-
-tus est de Spi- ri- tu San- - cto ex Ma-
-tus est de Spi- ri- tu San- - cto ex Ma-
-tus est de Spi- ri- tu San- - cto ex Ma-
-tus est de Spi- - ri- tu San- cto ex Ma-
54
-ri- a Vir- - gi- ne: et ho- - mo
-ri- a Vir- - gi- ne: et ho-
-ri- a Vir- - gi- ne: et ho-
-ri- - - a Vir- gi- ne: et
-ri- a Vir- - gi- ne: et ho- - mo

62
fa- - ctus est. Cru- ci- fi-
- mo fa- ctus est.
-mo fa- - ctus est. Cru- ci- fi- xus e- ti- am pro no- bis, e-
ho- mo fa- ctus est.
fa- ctus est.
68
[D1]
-xus e- ti- am pro no- bis: sub Pon- ti- o, sub Pon- ti-
[D3]
- ti- am, e- ti- am pro no- bis: sub Pon- ti- o, sub Pon- ti- o
B.c.
73
-o Pi- la- to pas- - sus, et se- pul- tus est, pas- sus et se- pul-
Pi- la- to pas- - sus, et se- pul- tus est, se-
78
[D1]
- tus, se- pul- tus est. Et re- sur- re- xit ter- ti- a di- - e,
[D3]
-pul- tus est. Et re- sur- re- xit ter- ti- a di- - e,
[BD]
Et re- sur- re- xit ter- ti- a di- e, se-
B.c.

83
se- cun- dum Scri- ptu- ras, Scri- ptu- ras. Et a- scen- dit in
se- cun- dum Scri- ptu- ras, se- cun- dum Scri- ptu- ras.
-cun- dum Scri- ptu- ras, se- cun- dum Scri- ptu- ras.
89
cae- lum, in cae- lum: se- det ad de- xte- ram, ad de-
Et a- scen- dit in cae- lum: se- det ad de- xte- ram, se- det ad de- xte-
Et a- scen- dit in cae- lum: se- det ad de- xte- ram, ad de- xte-
94
[D1]
- xte- ram Pa- tris.
[D2]
Et i- te- rum ven- tu- rus est cum glo- ri- a,
[D3]
-ram Pa- tris. Et i- te- rum ven- tu- rus est cum glo- ri- a,
[BD]
-ram Pa- tris. Et i- te- rum ven- tu- rus est cum glo- ri- a,
[B]
Et i- te- rum ven- tu- rus est cum glo- ri- a,
B.c.

100
ju- di- ca- re vi- vos, vi- vos et mor- tu- os: cu- jus re- gni non e- rit fi-
ju- di- ca- re vi- vos, vi- vos et mor- tu- os: cu- jus re- gni non e- rit fi-
ju- di- ca- re vi- vos et mor- tu- os: cu- jus re- gni non e- rit fi-
ju- di- ca- re vi- vos, vi- vos et mor- tu- os: cu- jus re- gni non e- rit fi-
106
Et in Spi- ri- tum San- ctum, Do- mi- num, et vi- vi- fi- can- tem: qui
-nis.
-nis.
-nis.
-nis.

112
ex Pa- tre Fi- li- o- que pro- ce- dit.
Qui cum Pa- tre et Fi- li-
Qui cum Pa- tre et Fi- li-
Qui cum Pa- tre et Fi- li-
Qui cum Pa- tre et Fi- li-
118
-o si- mul a- do- ra- tur, et con- glo- ri- fi- ca- - tur: qui lo- cu- tus
-o si- mul a- do- ra- tur, et con- glo- ri- fi- ca- tur: qui lo- cu- tus
-o si- mul a- do- ra- tur, et con- glo- ri- fi- ca- - tur: qui lo- cu-
-o si- mul a- do- ra- tur, et con- glo- ri- fi- ca- tur: qui lo- cu- tus

124
Et u- nam san- ctam ca- tho- li- cam et a- po- sto- li- cam Ec-
est per Pro- - phe- tas.
est per Pro- phe- tas. et a- po- sto- li- cam Ec-
- tus est per Pro- phe- tas.
est per Pro- phe- tas.
130
-cle- si- am.
Con- fi- te- or, con- fi- te- or u- num ba- pti- sma in re- mis- si- o-
-cle- si- am. Con- fi- te- or u- num ba- pti- sma in re- mis- si- o-
Con- fi- te- or, con- fi- te- or, con- fi- te- or u- num ba- pti- sma in re- mis- si- o-
Con- fi- te- or, con- fi- te- or u- num ba- pti- sma in re- mis- si- o-

136
Et ex- spe- cto re- sur- re- cti- o- nem mor- tu-
- nem pec- ca- to- rum.
-nem pec- ca- to- rum.
- nem pec- - ca- to- rum.
-nem pec- ca- to- rum.
141
-o- rum. Et vi- tam ven- tu- ri sae-
Et vi- tam ven- tu- ri sae- cu- li,
Et vi- tam ven- tu- ri, ven- tu- - ri sae- cu- li, a- men, sae-
Et vi- tam ven- tu- ri sae- cu- li, a- men, sae-
Et vi- tam ven- tu- ri, et vi- tam ven- tu- ri sae- cu-

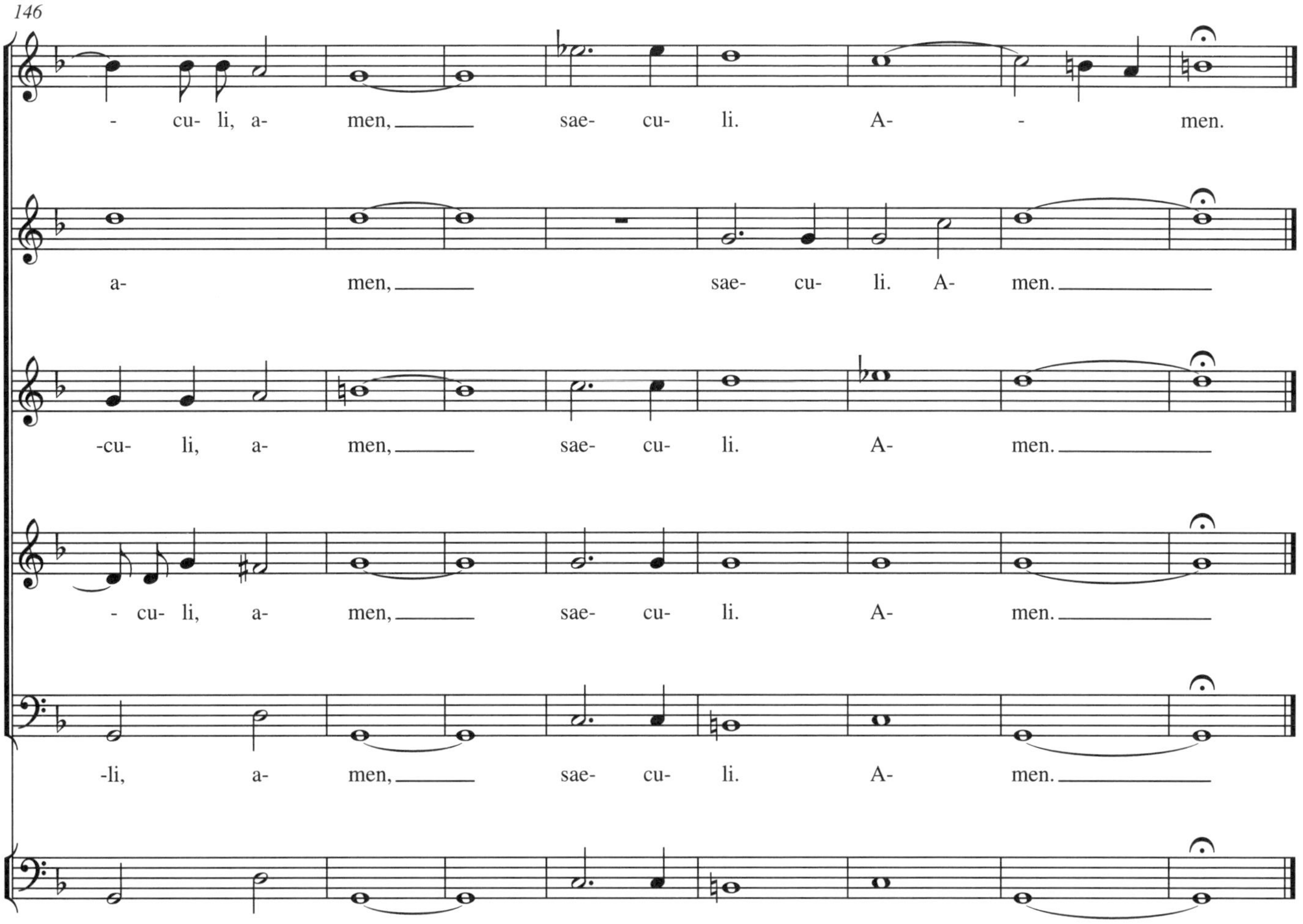

146
- cu- li, a- men, sae- cu- li. A- - men.
a- men, sae- cu- li. A- men.
-cu- li, a- men, sae- cu- li. A- men.
- cu- li, a- men, sae- cu- li. A- men.
-li, a- men, sae- cu- li. A- men.

Sanctus

[Dessus 1]
San- - - - - ctus, San- -
[Dessus 2]
[Dessus 3]
[Bas-dessus]
San- - - ctus, San-
[Basse]
San-
Basse continue

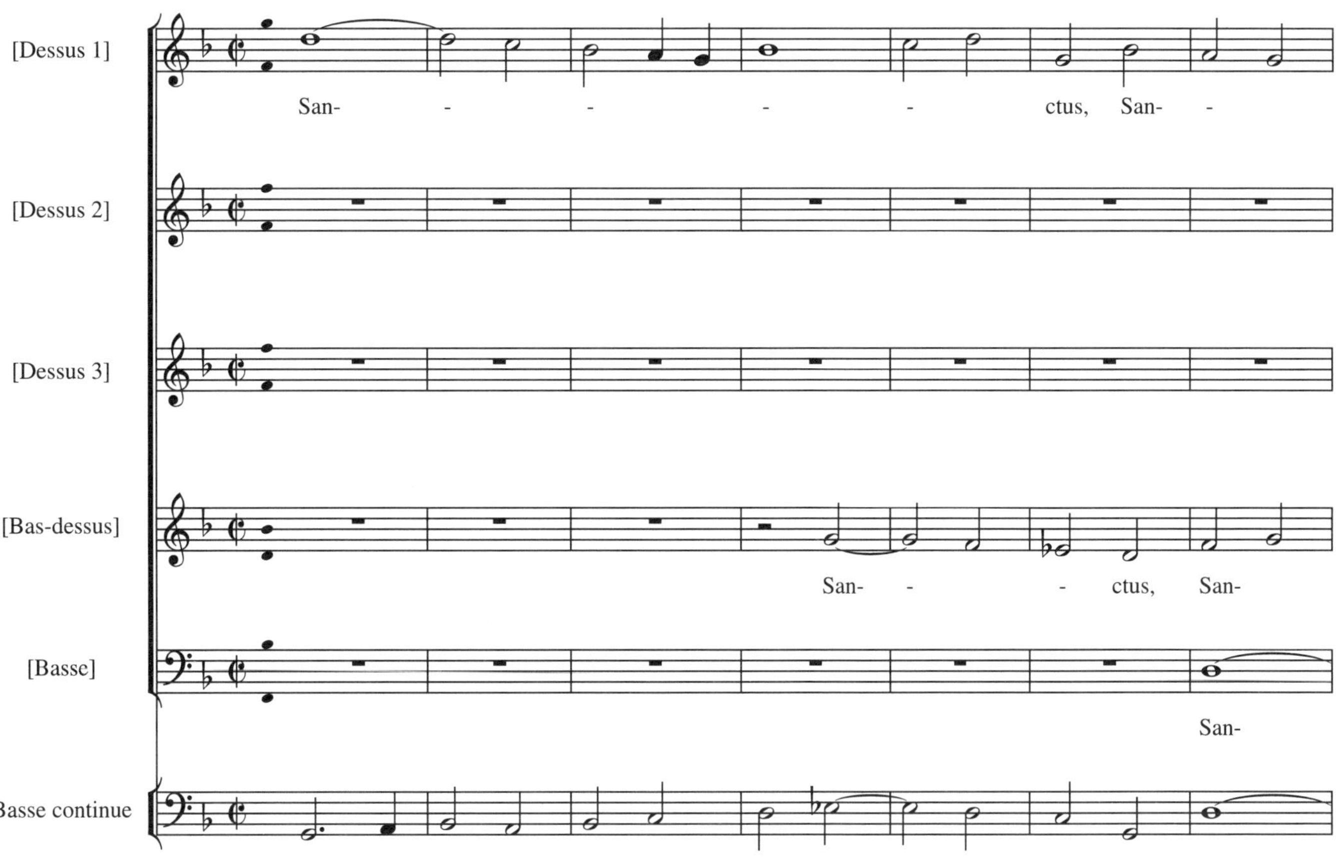

8
- - ctus,
San- - - ctus,
San- - - ctus, San- - - ctus,
- - - ctus, San- - ctus,
- - - ctus, San- ctus, San- -
16
San- - ctus Do- mi- nus De- us, De-
San- - ctus De- - us, Do- - mi- nus
San- - ctus Do- mi- nus De- us, Do- - mi- nus
San- - ctus Do- - mi- nus De- us, Do- - mi- nus
- - ctus Do- mi- nus De- us, Do- - mi- nus

24
- us Sa- - ba- oth. Ple- ni sunt cae- li et
De- us Sa- ba- oth. Ple- ni sunt cae- li, cae- li et
De- us Sa- ba- oth. Ple- ni sunt cae- li, cae- li et
De- us, De- - us Sa- ba- oth. cae- li et
De- us Sa- - ba- oth. Ple- ni sunt cae- li, cae- li et
33
ter- ra glo- - ri- a, glo- ri- a tu- a, glo- ri- a
ter- ra glo- ri- a tu- - a, glo- ri- a
ter- ra glo- - - ri- a tu- a, glo- - ri- a
ter- ra glo- - ri- a
ter- ra glo- - ri- a tu- a, glo- ri- a

41
tu- a. Ho- san- na in ex- cel- -
tu- a.
tu- a.
tu- a. Ho- san- na in ex- cel- - -
tu- a. Ho-
47
- sis, in ex- cel- sis, ho- san- na in ex- cel- sis, in ex- cel-
Ho- san- na in ex- cel- sis, in ex- cel-
Ho- san- na in ex- cel- sis, in ex- cel- sis, in ex- cel-
- sis, ho- san- na in ex- cel- sis, in ex- cel-
-san- na in ex- cel- sis, ho- san- na, ho- san- na in ex- cel-

52
-sis, ho-
-sis, ho- san- - na, ho- san-
-sis, ho- san- - na, ho- san- na in ex- cel- sis,
-sis, ho- san- - na in ex- cel- sis,
-sis, ho- san-
57
-san- na, ho- san- na in ex- cel- sis.
- na, ho- san- na, ho- san- na in ex- cel- sis.
ho- san- na in ex- cel- sis, ho- - san- na in ex- cel- sis.
ho san- na in ex- cel- - sis, in ex- cel- sis.
- na, ho- san- na in ex- cel- sis, ho- san- na in ex- cel- sis.

Agnus Dei

*See the editorial methods.

16
-re- re no- bis, no- bis,
no- bis pa- cem, pa- cem,
-di: mi- - se- re- re, mi- se-
do- - na no- bis, do- na
-di: mi- se- re-
do- na no-
-di: mi- - se- re- re, mi- se- re- re, mi- se-
do- - na no- bis, do- na no- bis, do- na
-di: mi- - se- re- re no- bis, mi- se- re-
do- - na no- bis pa- cem, do- na no-
24
mi- se- re- re no- - bis.
do- na no- bis pa- - cem.
-re- re no- - bis, mi- se- re- re no- bis.
no- bis pa- - cem, do- na no- bis pa- cem.
- re no- bis, mi- se- re- - re no- bis.
- bis pa- cem, do- na no- - bis pa- cem.
-re- re no- - bis, mi- se- re- re no- bis.
no- bis pa- - cem, do- na no- bis pa- cem.
- re no- bis, mi- se- re- re no- - bis.
- bis pa- cem, do- na no- bis pa- - cem.

Messe de Boesset du Tiers

Kyrie

15
-e e- le- - i- son.
-e e- le- - i- son.
-e, Ky- ri- e e- le- i- son.
-e e- le- - i- son.
17
Plain chant
Chri- ste e- le- i- son.
18
[D1]
Chri- ste e-
[D2]
[BD]
[B]
[B.c.]
19
-le- - i- son, e- le- i- son, e- le- - i-
Chri- ste e- le- - i- son, Chri- ste e- le- i-
Chri- ste e- le- i-
24
-son, e- le- - i- son.
-son, Chri-ste e- le- i- son.
-son, Chri- ste e- le- i- son.
27
Plain chant
Chri- ste e- le- i- son.
28
[D1]
[D2]
[BD]
Ky- ri-
[B]
[B.c.]

29
Ky- ri- e e- le- i- son, e- le- -
Ky- - ri- e e- le- i- son, e-
-e, Ky- ri- e e- le- i- son, Ky- ri- e e- le- -
Ky- ri- e e- le- i- son, e- le- -
34
- i- son.
-le- i- son.
- i- son.
- i- son.
36
Plain chant
Ky- ri- e e- le- i- son.
37
[D1]
Ky- ri- e e- le-
[D2]
[BD]
Ky-
[B]
[B.c.]
39
- i- son, e- le- - i- son, Ky- ri- e e- le- - i- son.
Ky- - ri- e, Ky- ri- e e- le- - i- son.
- ri- e e- le- i- son, Ky- ri- e, Ky- ri- e e- le- i- son.
Ky- - ri- e e- le- i- son, Ky- ri- e e- le- - i- son.

Gloria

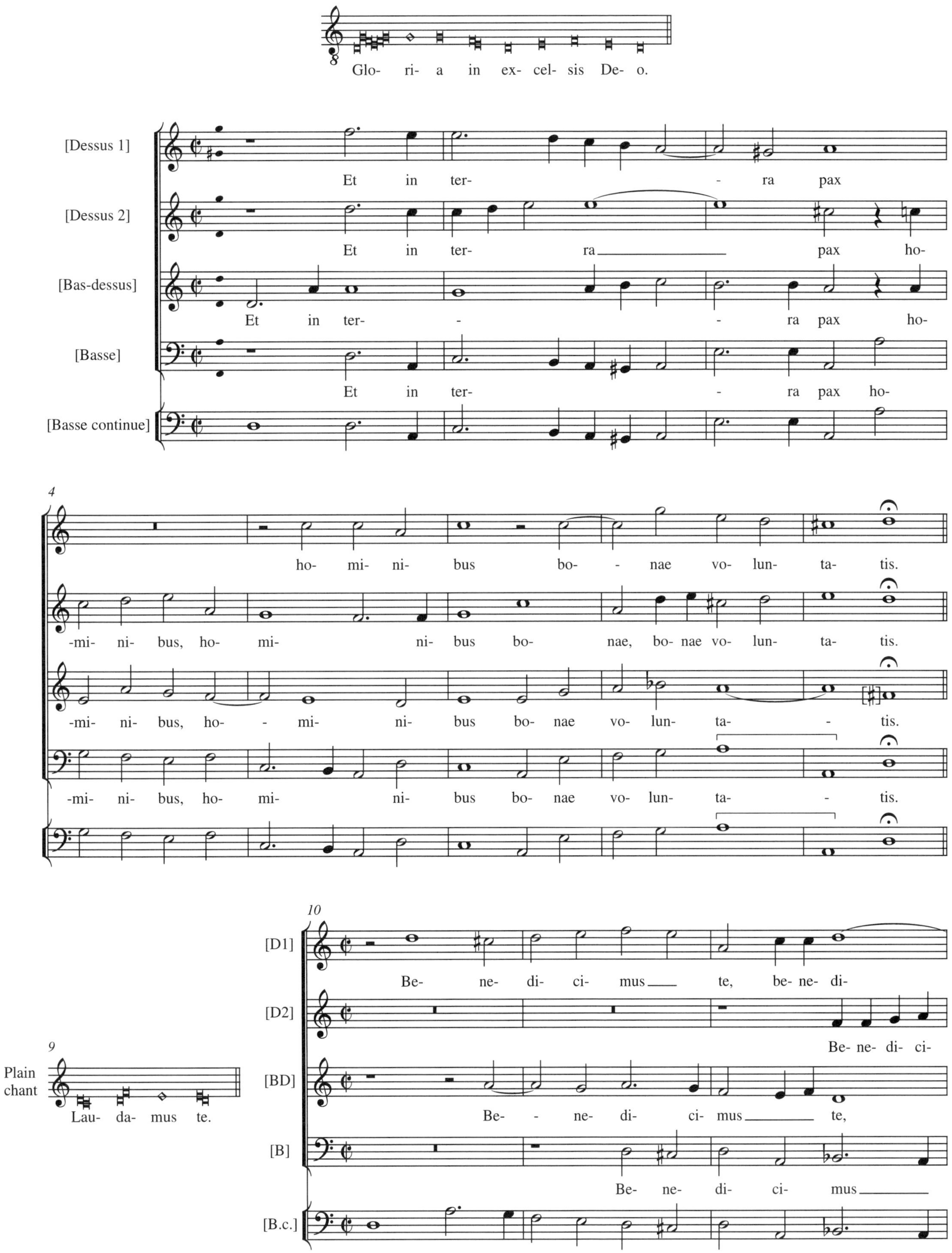

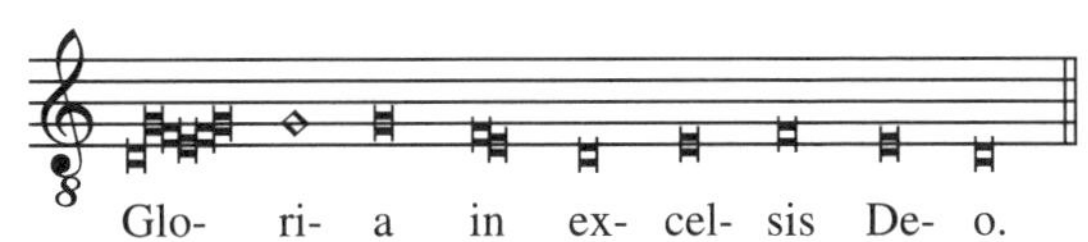

[Dessus 1]
Et in ter- - ra pax

[Dessus 2]
Et in ter- ra pax ho-

[Bas-dessus]
Et in ter- - - ra pax ho-

[Basse]
Et in ter- - ra pax ho-

[Basse continue]

4

ho- mi- ni- bus bo- - nae vo- lun- ta- tis.

-mi- ni- bus, ho- mi- ni- bus bo- nae, bo- nae vo- lun- ta- tis.

-mi- ni- bus, ho- - mi- ni- bus bo- nae vo- lun- ta- - tis.

-mi- ni- bus, ho- mi- ni- bus bo- nae vo- lun- ta- - tis.

13
- ci- mus te.
-mus te.
be- ne- di- ci- mus te.
te, be- ne- di- ci- mus te.
15
Plain chant
Ad- o- ra- mus te.
16
[D1]
Glo-
[D2]
[BD]
Glo- ri- fi-
[B]
[B.c.]
17
-ri- fi- ca- mus te, glo- - ri- fi- ca- - mus te.
Glo- ri- fi- ca- mus te.
-ca- mus te, glo- ri- fi- ca- mus te.
Glo- ri- fi- ca- mus te.
21
Plain chant
Gra- ti- as a- gi- mus ti- bi pro- pter ma- gnam glo- ri- am tu- am.
22
[D1]
[D2]
[BD]
Do-
[B]
Do- mi- ne
[B.c.]

23
De- - us Pa- ter om-
De- - us Pa- ter om-
-mi- ne De- - us, Rex cae- - le- stis, De- - us Pa- ter om-
De- us, De- - us, Rex cae- le- stis, De- us Pa- ter om-
28
-ni- po- tens, om- ni- po- tens.
-ni- po- tens, om- ni- po- tens.
-ni- po- tens, om- ni- po- tens.
-ni- po- tens, om- ni- po- tens.
30
Plain chant
Do- mi- ne Fi- li u- ni- ge- ni- te Je- su Chri- ste.
31
[D1]
Do- mi- ne De- - - us, A- gnus,
[D2]
A- - gnus De-
[BD]
Do- mi- ne De- us, A-
[B]
Do- mi- ne De- us, A-
[B.c.]

36
A- gnus De- i, Fi- - li- us Pa- - tris.
- i, Fi- li- us Pa- tris.
- gnus De- i, Fi- li- us, Fi- li- us Pa- tris.
- gnus De- i, Fi- li- us Pa- tris.
40
Plain chant
Qui tol- lis pec- ca- ta mun- di, mi- se- re- re no- bis.
41
[D1]
Qui tol- lis pec-
[D2]
Qui tol- lis pec- ca-
[BD]
Qui tol- - lis
[B]
Qui tol- lis pec-
[B.c.]
43
-ca- ta mun- di, sus- ci- pe de- pre- ca- ti-
-ta, pec- ca- ta mun- di, sus- ci- pe de- pre- ca- ti- o-
pec- ca- ta mun- di, sus- ci- pe de- pre- ca- ti-
-ca- ta mun- di, sus- ci- pe de- pre- ca- ti-

49
-o- nem no- stram.
-nem no- stram.
-o- nem no- stram.
-o- nem no- stram.
51
Plain chant
Qui se- des ad de- xte- ram Pa- tris, mi- se- re- re no- bis.
52
[D1]
Quo- ni- am, quo- ni- am tu so- lus san- ctus.
[D2]
Quo- ni- am tu so- lus, tu so- lus san- ctus.
[BD]
Quo- ni- am tu so- lus, tu so- lus san- ctus.
[B]
Quo- ni- am tu so- lus san- ctus.
[B.c.]
57
Plain chant
Tu so- lus Do- mi- nus.
58
[D1]
Tu so- lus Al- tis- si- mus, Al- tis-
[D2]
Tu so- lus Al-
[BD]
[B]
Tu so- lus Al- tis- si- mus, Al- tis- - si- mus,
[B.c.]

61
- si- mus, tu so- lus Al- tis- si- - mus, Je- - su Chri-
-tis- si- mus, tu so- lus Al- tis- - si- mus, Je- su Chri-
Tu so- lus, tu so- lus Al- tis- si- mus, Je- su
tu so- lus Al- tis- si- mus, Je- - su Chri- ste, Je- su
66
- ste.
-ste.
Chri- ste.
Chri- ste.
Plain chant
67
Cum San- cto Spi- ri- tu,
68
[D1]
In glo- ri-
[D2]
In glo- ri- a,
[BD]
In glo- - ri- a, in glo-
[B]
In glo- ri- a, in glo- ri- a, in
[B.c.]
71
-a De- - i Pa- - tris. A- men.
in glo- ri- a, in glo- ri- a De- i Pa- - tris. A- men.
- ri- a, in glo- ri- a De- - i Pa- tris. A- men.
glo- ri- a, in glo- ri- a De- - i Pa- tris. A- men.

Credo

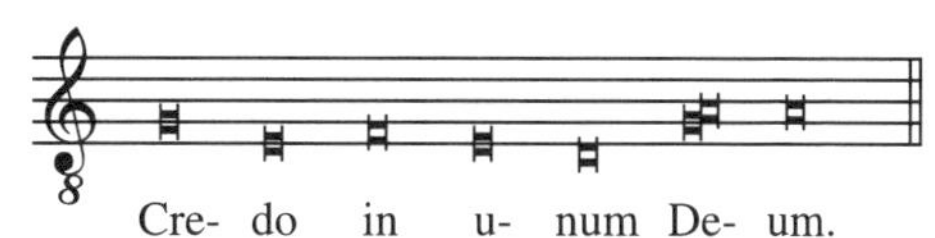

[Dessus 1] Pa- trem om- ni- po- ten- tem, om- ni- po- ten-

[Dessus 2] Pa- trem om- ni- po- ten- - tem,

[Bas-dessus] Pa- trem om- ni- po- ten-

[Basse] Pa- trem om- ni- po- ten- tem, —

[Basse continue]

5

-tem, om- ni- po- ten- tem.

om- ni- po- ten- tem.

-tem, om- ni- po- ten- tem.

— om- ni- po- ten- tem.

7

Plain chant: Fa- cto- rem cae- li et ter- rae

8

[D1] Vi- si- bi- li-

[D2] Vi- si- bi- li-

[BD] Vi- si- bi- li-

[B] Vi- si- bi- li-

[B.c.]

9

-um om- ni- um, et in- vi- si- bi- - li- um.

-um om- ni- um, et — in- vi- si- bi- - li- um.

-um om- - ni- um, et in- vi- si- bi- li- um.

-um om- ni- um, et in- vi- si- bi- - li- um.

13
Plain chant
Et in u- num Do- mi- num Je- sum Chri- stum, Fi- li- um De- i u- ni- ge- ni- tum.
14
[D1]
[D2]
[BD]
Et ex
[B]
[B.c.]
15
Et ex Pa- tre na- tum, et ex Pa- tre na- tum an- - te om- ni-
an- - te om- ni- a sae- cu-
Pa- tre na- - tum, na- - tum an-
Et ex Pa- - tre na- tum an- - te om- ni-
21
-a sae- cu- la, sae- cu- la.
-la, sae- cu- la, sae- cu- la.
- te om- ni- a sae- - cu- la.
-a sae- cu- la, sae- cu- la.
24
Plain chant
De- um de De- o, lu- men de

(24)
25
[D1]
[D2]
[BD]
[B]
[B.c.]
lu- mi- ne, De- um ve- rum de De- o ve- ro.
Ge- ni- tum, non fa- ctum,
27
con- sub- stan- ti- a- lem Pa- tri: per quem om- ni- a fa- cta sunt.
32
Plain chant
Qui pro- pter nos ho- mi- nes, et pro- pter no- stram sa- lu- tem de- scen- dit de cae- lis.
33
Et in- car-

34
-na- tus est de Spi- ri- tu San- cto ex
-na- tus est de Spi- - ri- tu San- - cto
-na- tus est de Spi- ri- tu San- cto ex Ma-
-na- tus est de Spi- ri- tu San- cto
40
Ma- ri- - a, ex Ma- ri- - a Vir- gi- ne:
ex Ma- ri- a Vir- gi-
-ri- a Vir- gi- ne, ex Ma- ri- a Vir- - gi- ne:
ex Ma- ri- a Vir- - gi- ne:
45
et ho- mo fa- ctus est.
-ne: et ho- mo fa- ctus est.
et ho- mo fa- ctus est.
et ho- mo fa- ctus est.
48
Plain chant
Cru- ci- fi- xus e- ti- am pro no- bis: sub Pon-

(48)
-ti- o Pi- la- to pas- sus, et se- pul- tus est.
49
[D1]
Et re- sur- re- xit, et re- sur- re-
[D2]
Et re- sur- re-
[BD]
Et
[B]
[B.c.]
52
- xit ter- ti- a di- - e, se- cun- dum Scri- ptu- ras, Scri- ptu-
-xit et re- - sur- re- - xit ter- ti- a di- e, se- cun- dum Scri-ptu-
re- sur- re- xit ter- ti- a di- e, ter- ti- a di- e, se- cun- dum Scri-
Et re- sur- re- xit ter- - ti- a di- e, se- cun- dum Scri- ptu-
58
-ras, Scri- ptu- ras.
-ras, Scri- ptu- ras.
-ptu- ras, Scri- ptu- ras.
-ras, Scri- ptu- ras.
60
Plain chant
Et a- scen- dit in cae- lum: se- det ad de- xte- ram Pa- tris.

61
[D1]
[D2]
[BD]
[B]
[B.c.]
Et i- te- rum ven- tu- rus est cum glo- ri- a, cum glo- ri-
Et i- te- rum ven- tu- rus est cum glo- ri- a, cum
Et i- te- rum ven- tu- rus est cum glo- ri- a, cum glo- ri-
Et i- te- rum ven- tu- rus est cum glo- ri- a, cum
67
-a, ju- di- ca- re vi- - vos, vi- vos et mor- tu- os: cu- jus
glo- ri- a, ju- di- ca- re vi- vos, vi- vos et mor- tu- os: cu- jus
-a, ju- di- ca- re vi- vos, vi- vos et mor- tu- os: cu- jus
glo- ri- a, ju- di- ca- re vi- vos, vi- vos et mor- tu- os: cu- jus
72
re- gni non e- rit fi- nis.
re- gni non e- rit fi- - nis.
re- gni non e- rit fi- nis.
re- gni non e- rit fi- nis.
75
Plain chant
Et in Spi- ri- tum San- ctum, Do- mi- num,

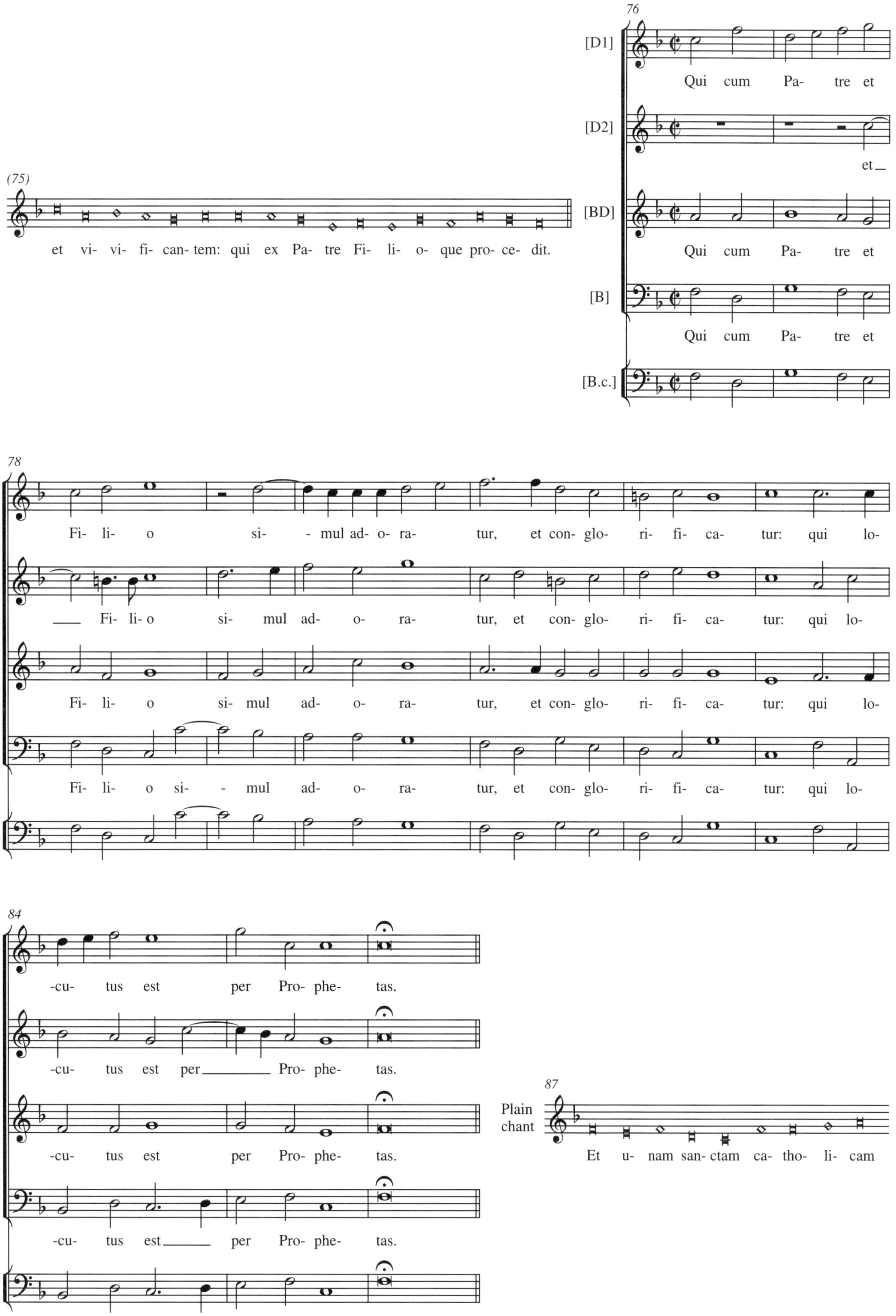

(75)
et vi- vi- fi- can- tem: qui ex Pa- tre Fi- li- o- que pro- ce- dit.
76
[D1]
Qui cum Pa- tre et
[D2]
et
[BD]
Qui cum Pa- tre et
[B]
Qui cum Pa- tre et
[B.c.]
78
Fi- li- o si- mul ad- o- ra- tur, et con- glo- ri- fi- ca- tur: qui lo-
Fi- li- o si- mul ad- o- ra- tur, et con- glo- ri- fi- ca- tur: qui lo-
Fi- li- o si- mul ad- o- ra- tur, et con- glo- ri- fi- ca- tur: qui lo-
Fi- li- o si- mul ad- o- ra- tur, et con- glo- ri- fi- ca- tur: qui lo-
84
-cu- tus est per Pro- phe- tas.
-cu- tus est per Pro- phe- tas.
-cu- tus est per Pro- phe- tas.
-cu- tus est per Pro- phe- tas.
87
Plain chant
Et u- nam san- ctam ca- tho- li- cam

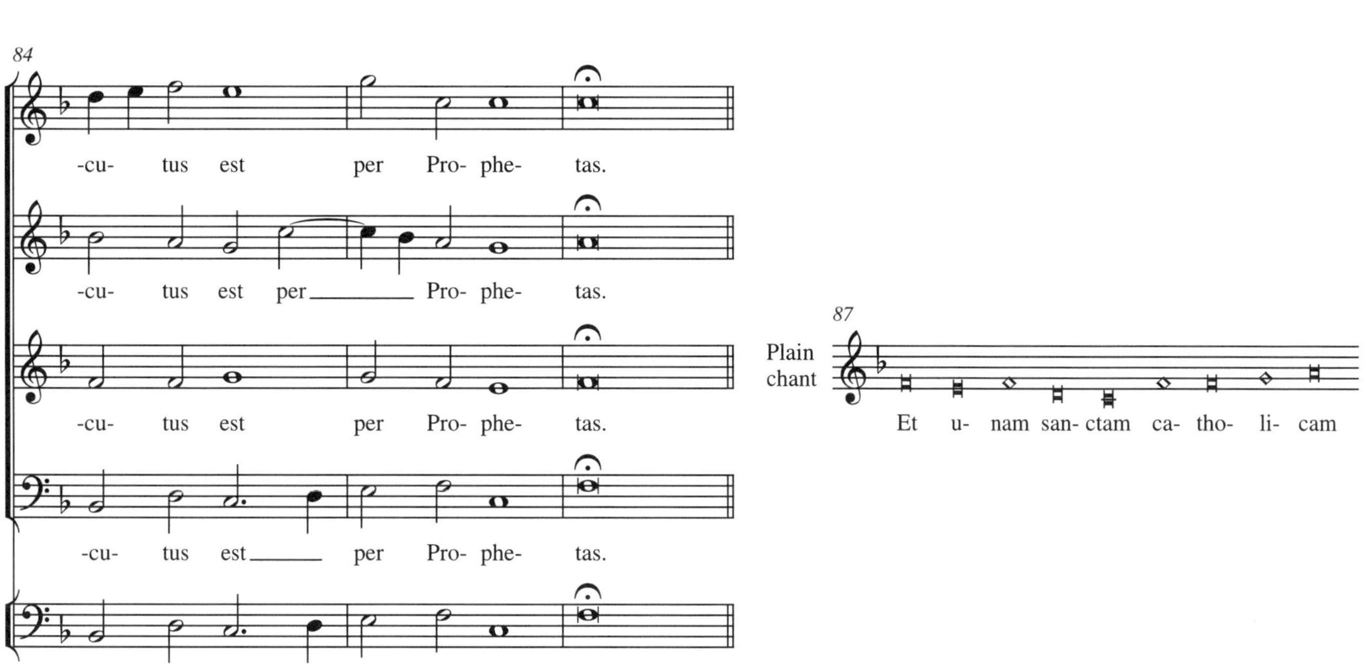

(87)
et a- po- sto- li- cam Ec- cle- si- am.
88
[D1]
[D2]
[BD]
[B]
[B.c.]
Con- fi- te- or, con- fi-
Con- fi- te- or, con- fi- te- or u- num ba-
91
- te- or u- num, u- num ba- pti- sma in re- mis- si- o- nem pec- ca-
Con- fi- te- or u- - num ba- pti- sma in re-mis- si- o- nem pec-ca-
-pti- sma in re-mis- si- o- nem pec-ca- to-
Con- fi- te- or u- num ba- pti- sma in re- mis- si- o- nem pec- ca-
96
-to- rum.
-to- rum.
- rum.
-to- rum.
Plain chant
98
Et ex- spe- cto re- sur- re- cti- o- nem mor- tu- o- rum.
99
Et

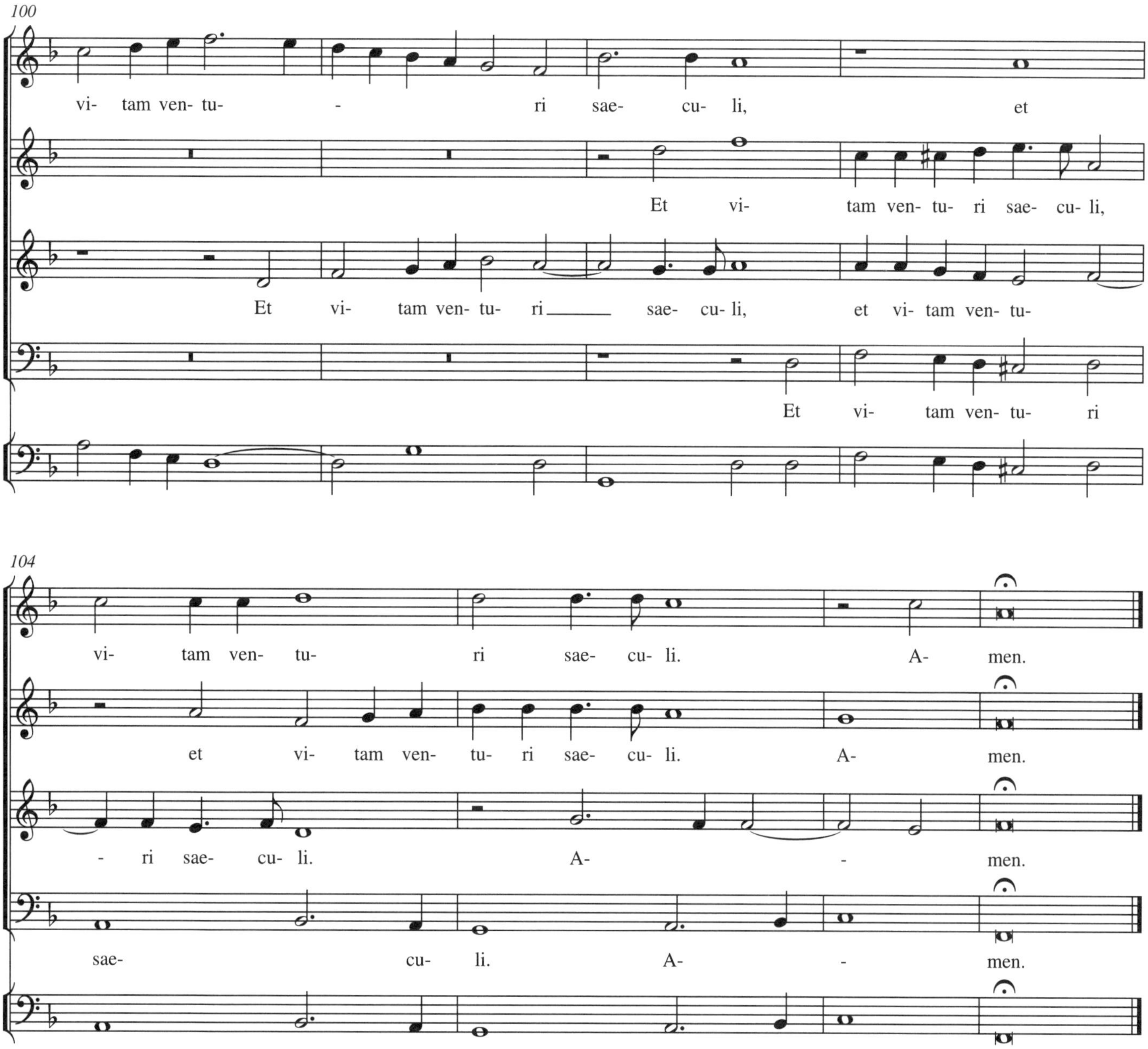

100
vi- tam ven- tu- - ri sae- cu- li, et
Et vi- tam ven- tu- ri sae- cu- li,
Et vi- tam ven- tu- ri sae- cu- li, et vi- tam ven- tu-
Et vi- tam ven- tu- ri
104
vi- tam ven- tu- ri sae- cu- li. A- men.
et vi- tam ven- tu- ri sae- cu- li. A- men.
- ri sae- cu- li. A- - men.
sae- cu- li. A- - men.

Sanctus

[Dessus 1]
[Dessus 2]
[Bas-dessus]
[Basse]
[Basse continue]
San- - - ctus.
San- - ctus, San- - ctus.
San- - - - ctus, San- ctus.
San- - - ctus, San- - ctus.

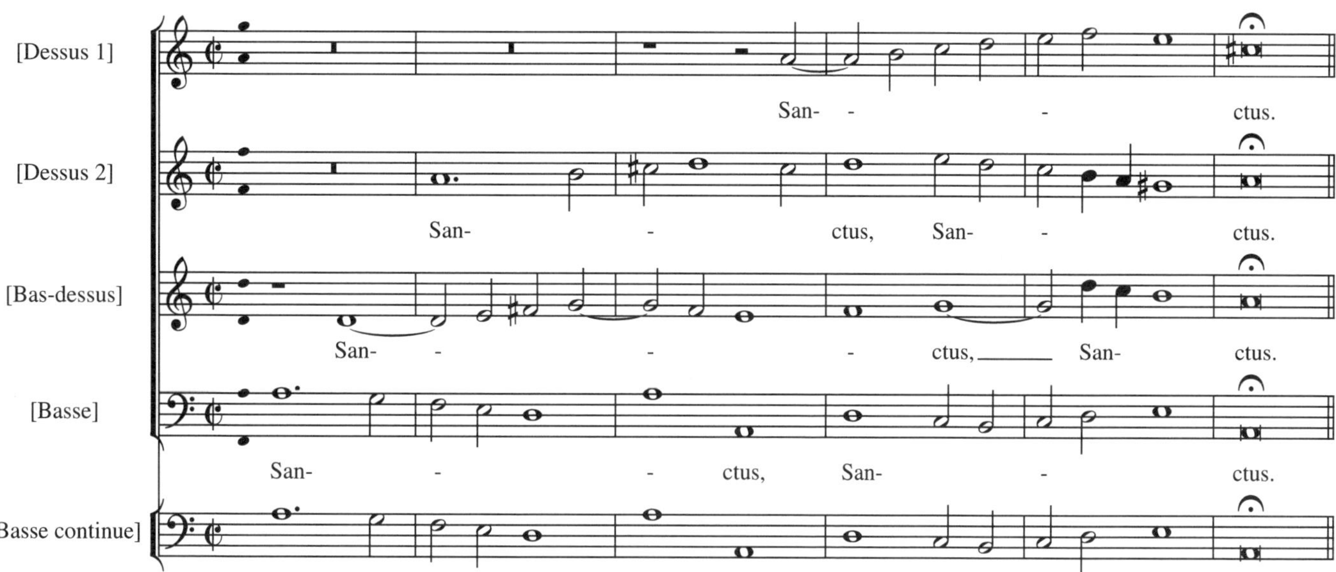

8
[D1]
San- ctus, San- - ctus, San-
[D2]
San- ctus, San- -
7
Plain chant
San- ctus
[BD]
San- ctus, San- - ctus,
[B]
[B.c.]
12
- ctus, San- - ctus.
- ctus, San- - ctus.
San- ctus, San- - ctus.
San- ctus, San- ctus, San- ctus.
15
Plain chant
San- ctus Do- mi- nus De- us Sa- ba- oth.
16
[D1]
Ple- ni sunt cae- li et ter- ra glo- - ri- a
[D2]
Ple- ni sunt cae- li et ter- ra glo- - ri- a
[BD]
Ple- ni sunt cae- li et ter- ra glo- - ri- a, glo-
[B]
Ple- ni sunt cae- li et ter- ra glo- - ri- a
[B.c.]

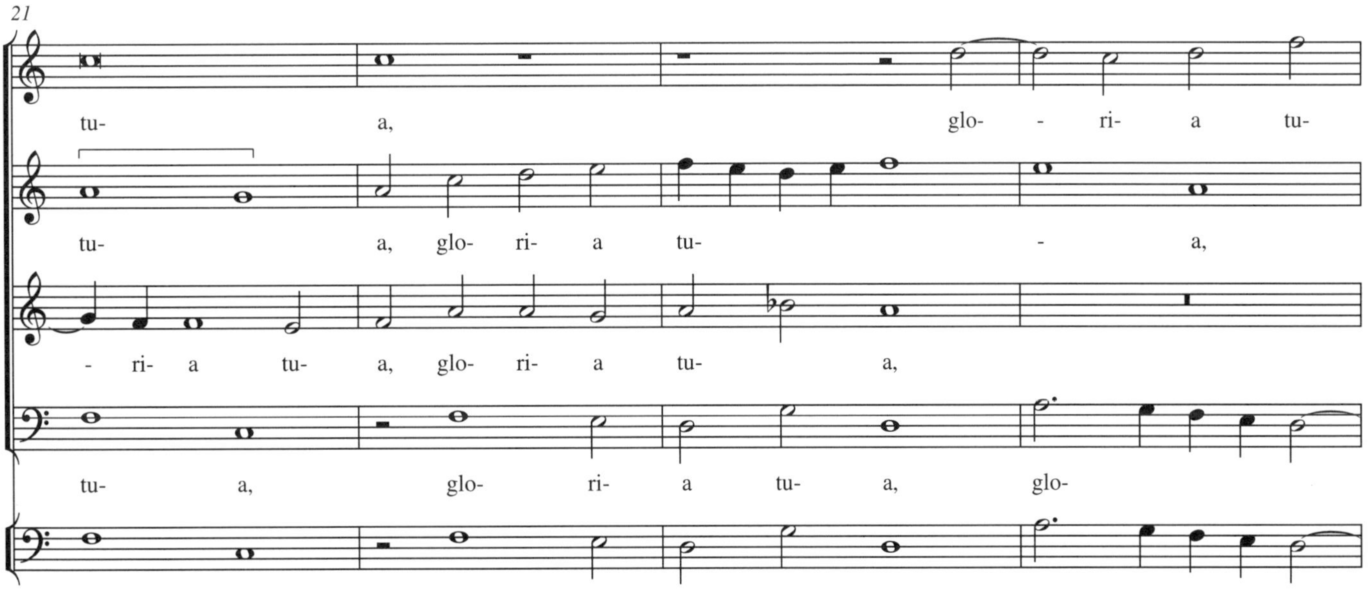

21
tu- a, glo- - ri- a tu-
tu- a, glo- ri- a tu- - a,
- ri- a tu- a, glo- ri- a tu- a,
tu- a, glo- ri- a tu- a, glo-

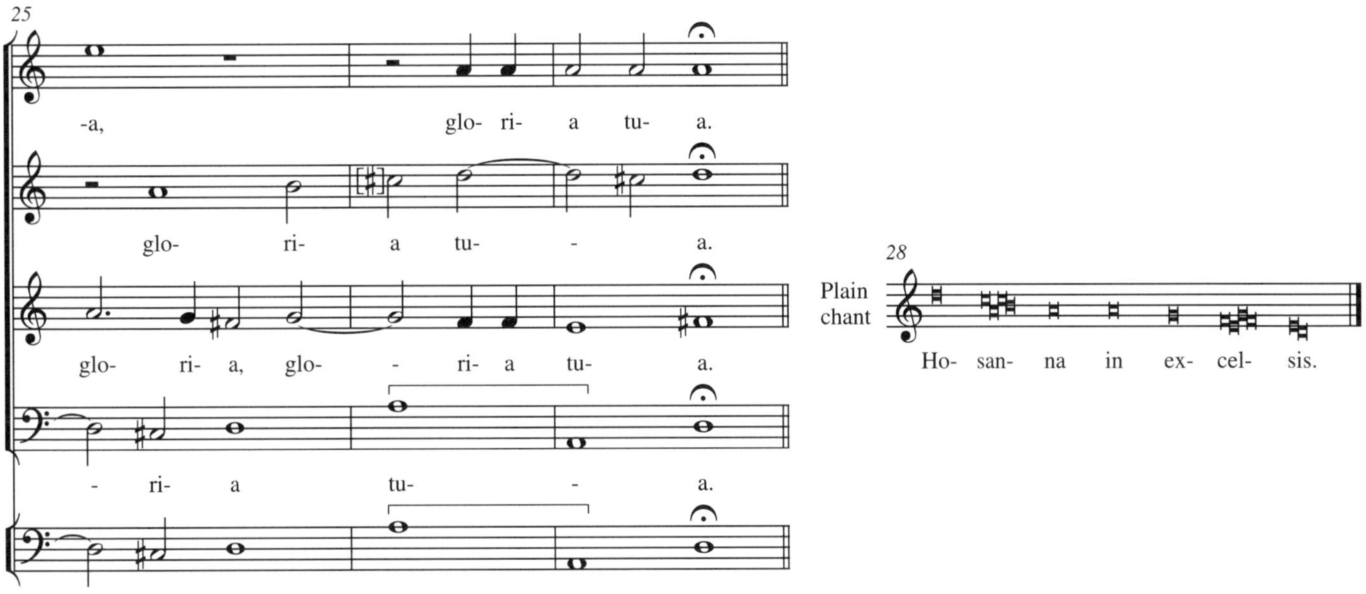

25
-a, glo- ri- a tu- a.
glo- ri- a tu- - a.
glo- ri- a, glo- - ri- a tu- a.
- ri- a tu- - a.
28
Plain chant
Ho- san- na in ex- cel- sis.

Agnus Dei

[Dessus 1]
[Dessus 2]
[Bas-dessus]
[Basse]
[Basse continue]
A- - gnus, A- - gnus
A- - gnus De- i, A- gnus
A- gnus
A- - gnus De-

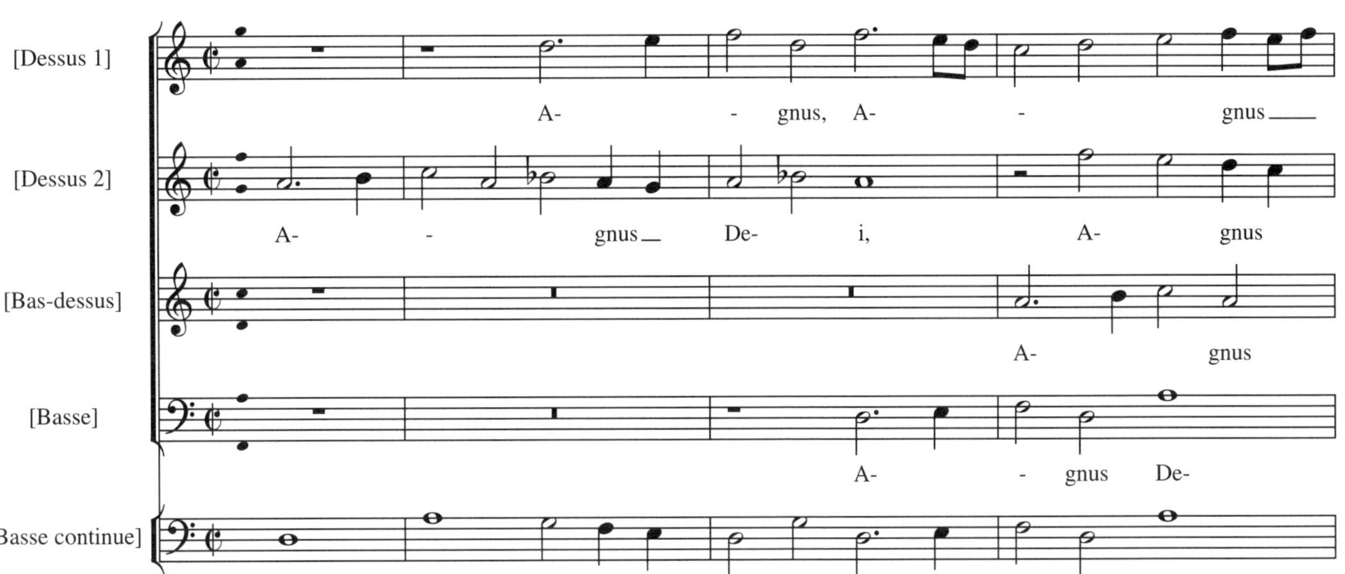

5
De- i, qui tol- lis, qui tol- lis pec- ca- ta mun- di:
De- i, qui tol- lis, qui tol- lis pec- ca- ta mun- di:
De- i, qui tol- lis, qui tol- lis pec- ca- ta mun- di:
- i, qui tol- lis, qui tol- lis pec- ca- ta mun- di:
10
mi- se- re- re
mi- se- re- re no- bis, mi- se- re- re
mi- se- re- re no- bis, mi- - se- re- re no- - bis, mi- se- re-
mi- se- re- re no- bis, mi- se- re- re, mi- se- re-
15
no- bis.
no- bis.
-re no- bis.
- re no- bis.
17
Plain chant
A- gnus De- i, qui tol- lis pec- ca- ta mun- di: mi- se- re- re no- bis.

*See the editorial methods.

Messe à 4 du 11e mode

Kyrie

16
-son, Chri- ste e- le- i- son, Chri- ste e- le- - i- son.
- - i- son, Chri- ste e- le- - i- son.
- i- son, Chri- ste e- le- - - i- son.
22
[D1]
Ky- ri- e e- le- - i- son, Ky- ri- e e-
[D2]
Ky- - ri- e
[HC]
Ky- ri- e, Ky- - ri- e e- le- i- son, Ky- ri- e e-
[B]
Ky- ri- e e- le- - i- son, Ky- ri- e e-
B.c.
27
-le- - i- son, Ky- ri- e e- le- i-
e- le- - i- son, Ky- ri- e e- le- i-
-le- - i- son, Ky- ri- e e- le- i-
-le- i- son, Ky- - ri- e e- le- i-

Gloria

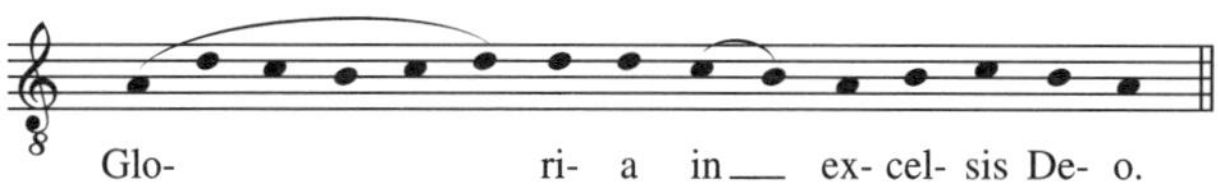

Glo- ri- a in ex- cel- sis De- o.

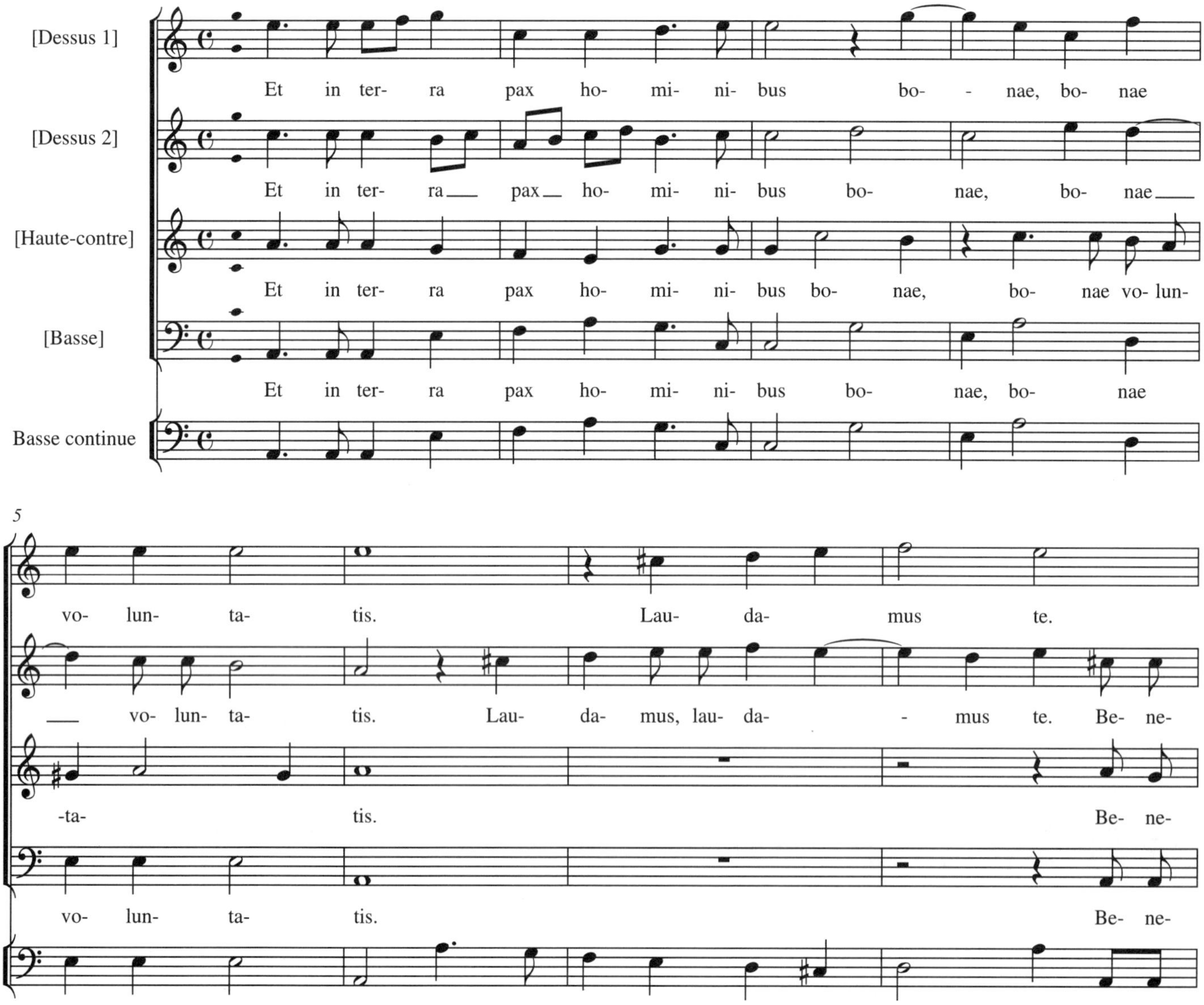

[Dessus 1] Et in ter- ra pax ho- mi- ni- bus bo- - nae, bo- nae

[Dessus 2] Et in ter- ra pax ho- mi- ni- bus bo- nae, bo- nae

[Haute-contre] Et in ter- ra pax ho- mi- ni- bus bo- nae, bo- nae vo- lun-

[Basse] Et in ter- ra pax ho- mi- ni- bus bo- nae, bo- nae

Basse continue

5

vo- lun- ta- tis. Lau- da- mus te.

vo- lun- ta- tis. Lau- da- mus, lau- da- - mus te. Be- ne-

-ta- tis. Be- ne-

vo- lun- ta- tis. Be- ne-

9
Be- ne- di- ci- mus te. Ad- o- ra- mus te. Glo-
-di- ci- mus, be- ne- di- ci- mus te. Ad- o- ra- - mus te.
-di- ci- mus, be- ne- di- ci- mus te. Ad- o- ra- mus te. Glo- ri- fi-
-di- ci- mus, be- ne- di- ci- mus te. Ad- o- ra- mus te.
14
-ri- fi- ca- mus te. Gra- ti- as, gra- ti- as a- gi- mus ti- bi pro- pter
Gra- ti- as, gra- ti- as a- - gi- mus ti- bi pro- pter
-ca- mus te. Gra- - ti- as, gra- ti- as a- gi- mus, a- gi- mus ti- bi pro- pter
Gra- ti- as, gra- ti- as a- gi- mus, a- gi- mus ti- bi pro- pter
19
ma- gam glo- - ri- am tu- am. Do- mi- ne De-
ma- gnam glo- ri- am tu- am. Do- mi- ne De- - us,
ma- gnam glo- ri- am tu- am.
ma- gnam glo- ri- am tu- am.

24
- us, Rex cae- le- stis, De- - us Pa- ter, Pa- - ter om-ni- po-
Rex ___ cae- le- - stis, De- - us Pa- ter om- ni- po-
29
-tens. Do- mi- ne Fi- li u- ni- ge- - ni- te
-tens. Do- mi- ne Fi- - li, Fi- li u- ni- ge- ni- te
Do- - mi- ne, Do- mi- ne Fi- li u- ni- ge- ni- te
Do- - mi- ne Fi- li u- ni- ge- ni- te, u- ni- ge- ni- te
34
Je- su Chri- ste, Je- su ___ Chri- ste. Do-
Je- su Chri- - ste, Je- su Chri- ste.
Je- su Chri- ste, Je- - su Chri- ste. Do- mi-
Je- su Chri- ste, Je- su Chri- ste.

40
- mi- ne De- - us, Do- mi- ne De- us, A-
Do-mi- ne, Do-mi- ne De- us, A- gnus,
-ne De- us, Do- - mi- ne De- - us, De- us, A-
Do- mi- ne De- us, A- - gnus, A- gnus
45
- gnus De- i, Fi- - li- us Pa- tris. Qui tol-
A- gnus De- i, Fi- li- us Pa- tris. Qui tol-
-gnus De- i, Fi- - li- us Pa- - tris. Qui tol-
De- i, Fi- - li- us Pa- tris. Qui tol-
52
-lis pec- ca- ta mun- di, mi- - se- re- - re no-
- lis pec- ca- - ta mun- di, mi- se- re- re, mi- - se- re- - re no-
-lis pec- ca- ta mun- di, mi- - se- re- re, mi- - se- re-
-lis pec- ca- ta mun- di, mi- - se- re- - re, mi- se- re-

58
-bis, mi- se- re- re no- - bis. Qui tol- lis pec- ca-
-bis, mi- se- re- - re no- bis.
-re, mi- se- re- re, mi- se- re- re no- bis. Qui tol- lis pec-
-re, mi- se- re- re no- bis.
64
-ta mun- di, sus- ci- pe de- pre- ca- ti- o- nem no- stram. Qui
sus- ci- pe de- pre- ca- ti- o- nem no- stram.
-ca- ta mun- di, sus- ci- pe de- pre- ca- ti- o- - nem no- stram.
sus- ci- pe de- pre- ca- ti- o- - nem no- stram.
70
se- des, qui se- des ad de- xte- ram Pa- tris, ad de-xte-ram Pa- -
Qui se- des, qui se- des ad de- xte- ram, ad de-xte- ram, ad de- xte- ram Pa-

76
-tris, mi- se- re- re no- bis, mi- se- re- re no- bis.
mi- se- re- re no- - bis, mi- - se- re- re no- bis.
-tris, mi- se- re- re no- - bis, mi- se- re- re no- bis.
mi- se- re- re no- bis, mi- se- re- re no- bis.
82
Quo- ni- am tu so- lus san- ctus, quo- ni- am tu so- lus san- ctus. Tu so- lus
Quo- ni- am tu so- lus, tu so- lus san- ctus. Tu
Tu so- lus Do-
Tu so- lus Do- mi-
87
Do- mi- nus, tu so- lus Do- mi- nus, tu so- lus Do- mi- nus, tu so- lus Do- mi-
so- lus Do- mi- nus, Do- mi- nus, tu so- lus Do- - mi- nus. Tu so-
- mi- nus, tu so- - lus Do- mi- nus.
-nus, tu so- lus, tu so- lus Do- mi- nus.

92
-nus. Tu so- lus Al- tis- si- mus, Je- su Chri-
-lus, tu so- lus Al- tis- si- mus, Je- su Chri- ste, Je- su Chri-
Tu so- lus Al- tis- si- mus, Je- su Chri- ste, Je-
Tu so- lus Al- tis- si- mus, Je- su Chri- ste, Je- - su Chri-
97
-ste. Cum San- cto Spi- ri- tu, cum San- cto Spi- ri- tu, in glo- ri-
- ste. Cum San- cto Spi- ri- tu, Spi- ri- tu, in glo- ri-
-su Chri- ste. Cum San- cto Spi- ri- tu, in glo- ri-
-ste. Cum San- cto Spi- ri- tu, in glo- ri-
102
-a, in glo- - ri- a, in glo- ri- a De- i Pa- - tris. A- men.
-a, in glo- ri- a De- - i Pa- tris, Pa- tris, De- i Pa- - tris. A- men.
-a, in glo- ri- a De- i Pa- tris. A- men.
-a, in glo- ri- a De- i Pa- - tris. A- men.

Credo

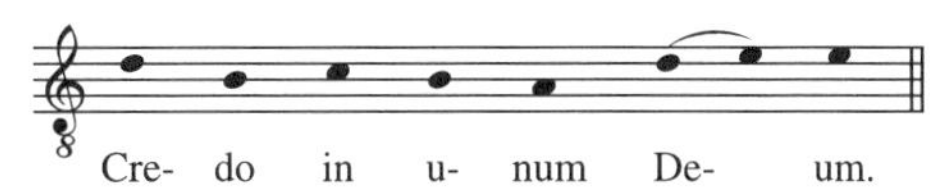

[Dessus 1] Pa- trem om- ni- po- ten- tem, fa- cto- rem cae- li et ter- rae,

[Dessus 2] fa- cto- rem cae- li et ter- rae,

[Haute-contre] fa- cto- rem cae- li et ter- rae,

[Basse] fa- cto- rem cae- li et ter- rae,

Basse continue

6

vi- si- bi- li- um om- - ni- um, et in- vi- si- bi- li- um. Et in

Et in u- num

Et in u- num

Et in u- num

11

u- num Do- mi- num Je- sum Chri- stum, Fi- - li- um De-

Do- mi- num Je- sum Chri- stum, Fi- - li- um De-

Do- mi- num Je- sum Chri- stum, Fi- - li- um De-

Do- mi- num Je- sum Chri- stum, Fi- li- um De-

16
- i u- ni- ge- ni- tum.
- i u- ni- ge- ni- tum. Et ex Pa- tre na- tum an- te om- ni-
- i u- ni- ge- ni- tum.
- i u- ni- ge- ni- tum.
21
De- um de De- o, lu- men, lu- men
-a sae- cu- la. De- um de De- - o, lu- men, lu- men
De- um de De- o, lu-
De- um de De- o, lu- men de lu- mi- ne, lu-
26
de lu- mi- ne, Ge- ni-
de lu- mi- ne, De- um ve- rum de De- o ve- ro. Ge- ni-
-men de lu- mi- ne, Ge- ni-
-men de lu- mi- ne. Ge- ni-

31
-tum, non fa- ctum, con- sub- stan- ti- a- - lem Pa- tri, con- sub-
-tum, non fa- ctum, con- sub- stan- ti- a- lem Pa- tri, con- sub-
-tum, non fa- - ctum, con- sub- stan- ti-
-tum, non fa- ctum, con- sub- stan- ti- a- - lem Pa- tri, con- sub-
36
-stan- ti- a- lem Pa- tri: per quem om- ni- a fa- cta sunt.
-stan- ti- a- lem Pa- tri: per quem om- ni- a fa- cta sunt.
-a- lem Pa- - tri: per quem om- ni- a, om- ni- a fa- cta sunt.
-stan- ti- a- - lem Pa- tri: per quem om- ni- a fa- cta sunt.
41
[D1]
Qui pro- pter nos ho- mi- nes, et pro- pter no- stram sa- lu-
B.c.
46
-tem de- scen- - dit, de- scen- dit de cae-

51
[D1]
[D2]
[HC]
[B]
B.c.
- lis. Et in- car- na- tus est de
Et in- car- na- tus est de Spi- ri-
Et in- car- na- tus est de Spi- ri-
Et in- car- na- tus est de Spi- ri-
57
Spi- ri- tu San- cto ex Ma- ri- a Vir- gi- ne: et ho- mo, et
-tu San- cto ex Ma- ri- a Vir- gi- ne: et ho- mo,
-tu San- cto ex Ma- ri- a Vir- gi- ne: et ho- mo
-tu San- cto ex Ma- ri- a Vir- gi- ne: et ho- mo
63
ho- mo fa- ctus est. Cru- ci- fi- xus e- - ti-
et ho- mo fa- ctus est. Cru- ci- fi-
fa- - ctus est.
fa- ctus est.

68
[D1]
[D2]
B.c.
-am pro no- bis: sub Pon- ti- o Pi- la- to, Pi- la-
-xus e- ti- am pro no- - bis: sub Pon- ti- o Pi-
73
- to pas- sus, et se- pul- tus est, se- pul- tus est.
-la- to pas- sus, et se- pul- tus est. Et
78
Et re- sur- re- xit ter- ti- a di- e, se- cun-
re- sur- re- - xit ter- - ti- a di- e, se- cun- dum Scri- ptu- ras,
83
-dum Scri- ptu- ras, Scri- ptu- ras. Et a- scen- dit in cae- lum: se-
se- cun- dum Scri- ptu- ras. Et a- scen- dit in cae-
88
-det, se- det ad de- xte- ram, ad de- xte- ram Pa- tris.
-lum: se- det ad de- xte- ram, ad de- xte- ram Pa- tris.

93
[D1]
Et i- te- rum ven- tu- rus est cum glo- ri- a, cum glo- ri- a, cum
[D2]
Et i- te- rum ven- tu- rus est cum glo- ri- a, cum glo- ri- a, cum glo- ri-
[HC]
Et i- te- rum ven- tu- rus est cum glo- ri- a, cum glo- ri-
[B]
Et i- te- rum ven- tu- rus est cum glo- ri- a, cum glo- ri-
B.c.
98
glo- ri- a, ju- di- ca- re vi- vos et mor- tu- os: cu- jus re- gni non
-a, ju- di- ca- re vi- vos et mor- tu- os: cu- jus re- gni non
-a, ju- di- ca- re vi- vos et mor- tu- os: cu- jus re- gni non
-a ju- di- ca- re vi- vos et mor- tu- os: cu- jus re- gni non
103
e- rit fi- nis.
e- rit fi- nis. Et in Spi- ri- tum San- ctum, Do- mi- num, et vi- vi- fi-
e- rit fi- nis.
e- rit fi- nis.

109
Qui cum Pa- tre et
-can- tem: qui ex Pa- tre Fi- li- o- que pro- ce- dit. Qui cum Pa- tre et
Qui cum Pa- tre et
Qui cum Pa- tre et
115
Fi- li- o si- mul ad- o- ra- tur, et con- glo- ri- fi- ca-
Fi- li- o si- mul ad- o- ra- tur, et con- glo- ri- fi- ca- -
Fi- li- o si- mul ad- o- ra- tur, et con- glo- ri- fi- ca-
Fi- li- o si- mul ad- o- ra- tur, et con- glo- ri- fi- ca-
120
-tur: qui lo- cu- - tus est per Pro- phe- tas. Et u- nam san- ctam ca-
-tur: Et u- nam san- ctam ca-
-tur: Et u- nam san- ctam ca-
-tur: Et u- nam san- ctam ca-

126
-tho- li- cam et a- po- sto- li- cam Ec- cle- - si- am.
-tho- li- cam et a- po- sto- li- cam Ec- cle- si- am. Con- fi- te-
-tho- li- cam et a- po- sto- li- cam Ec- cle- si- am.
-tho- li- cam et a- po- sto- li- cam Ec- cle- - si- am.
131
-or u- num ba- pti- sma in re- mis- si- o- nem pec- ca- to-
136
Et ex- spe- cto re- sur- re- cti- o- nem mor- - tu- o-
-rum. Et ex- spe- cto re- - sur- re- cti- o- - nem mor- tu- o-
Et ex- spe- cto re- sur- re- cti- o- - nem mor- tu- o-
Et ex- spe- cto re- sur- re- cti- o- - nem mor- tu- o-

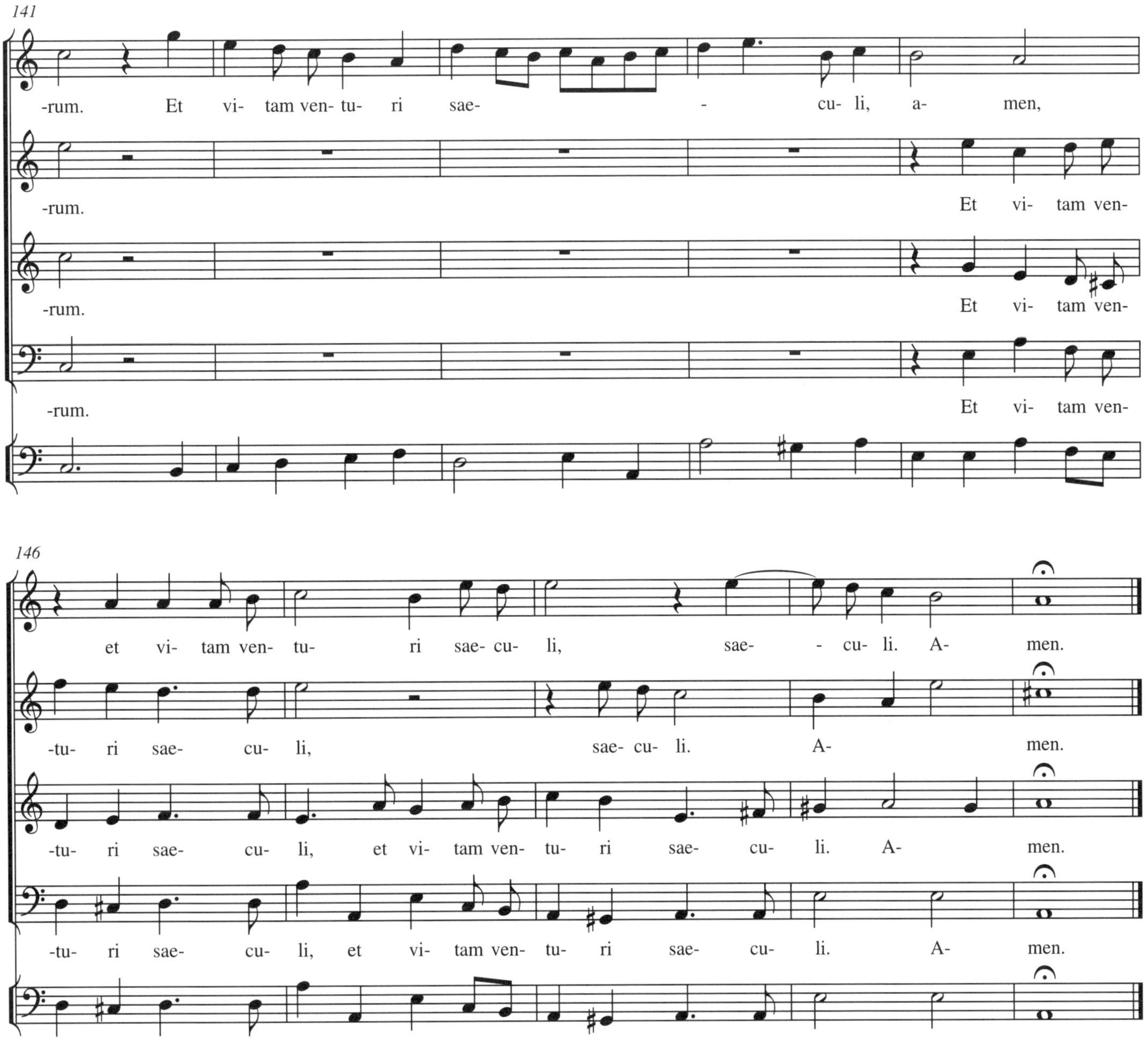

141
-rum. Et vi- tam ven- tu- ri sae- - cu- li, a- men,
-rum. Et vi- tam ven-
-rum. Et vi- tam ven-
-rum. Et vi- tam ven-
146
et vi- tam ven- tu- ri sae- cu- li, sae- - cu- li. A- men.
-tu- ri sae- cu- li, sae- cu- li. A- men.
-tu- ri sae- cu- li, et vi- tam ven- tu- ri sae- cu- li. A- men.
-tu- ri sae- cu- li, et vi- tam ven- tu- ri sae- cu- li. A- men.

Sanctus

[Dessus 1]
[Dessus 2]
[Haute-contre]
[Basse]
Basse continue
San- - ctus, San-
San- - - ctus, San-
San-

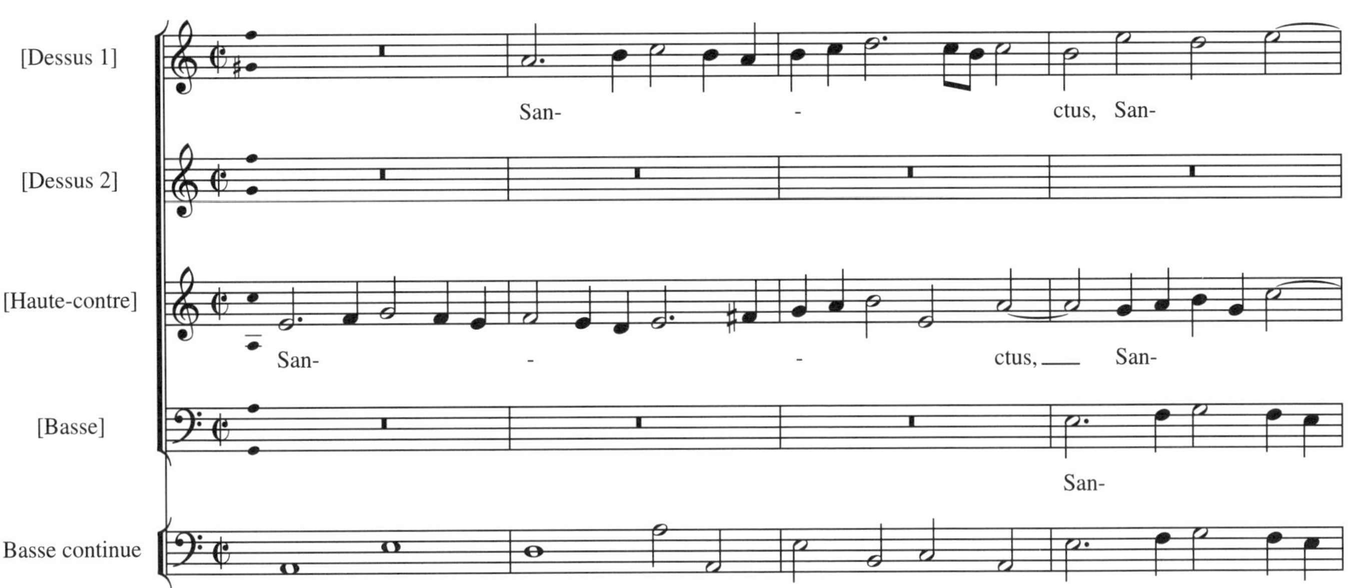

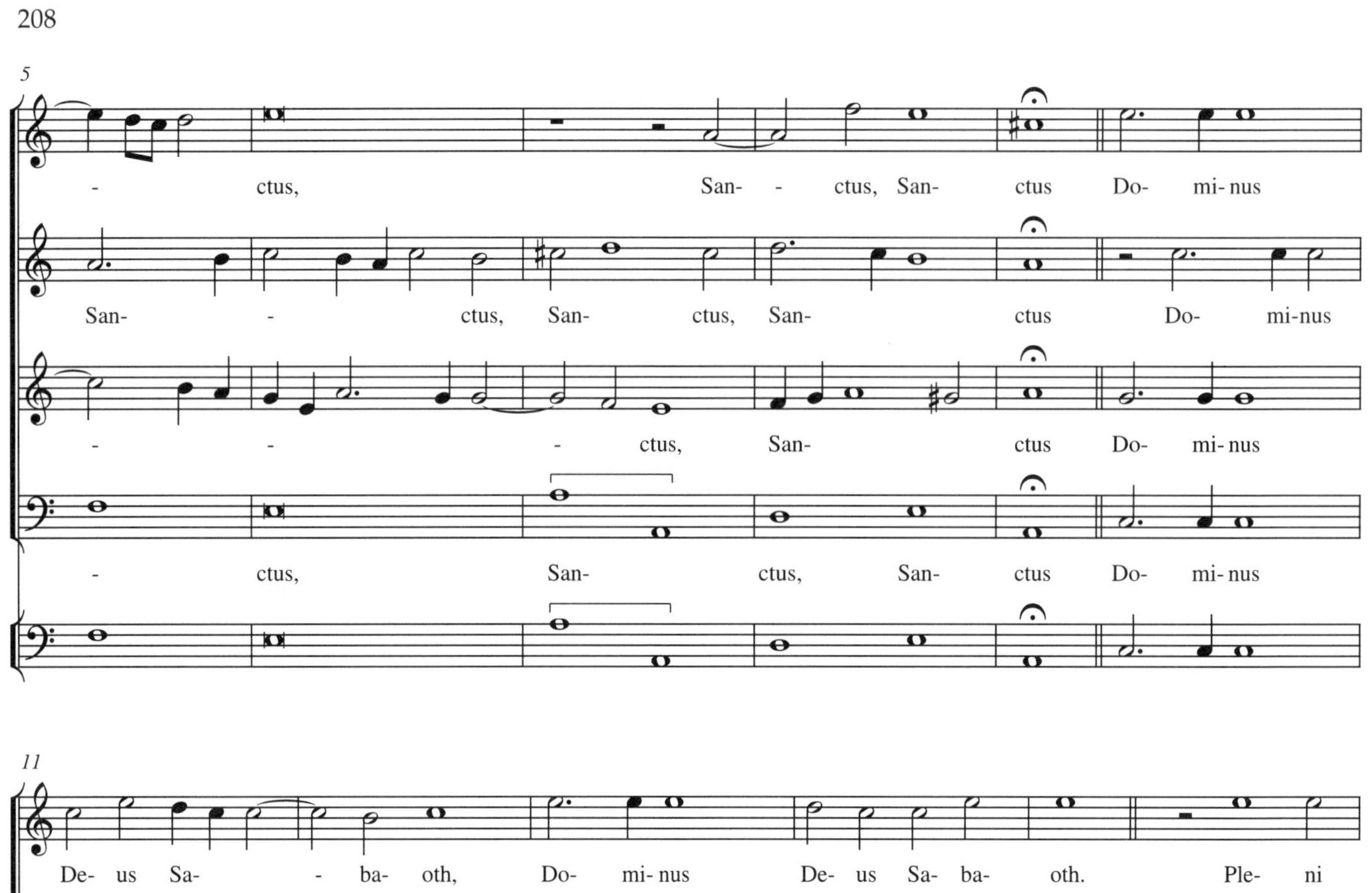
5
- ctus, San- - ctus, San- ctus Do- mi- nus
San- - ctus, San- ctus, San- ctus Do- mi- nus
- - - ctus, San- ctus Do- mi- nus
- ctus, San- ctus, San- ctus Do- mi- nus

11
De- us Sa- - ba- oth, Do- mi- nus De- us Sa- ba- oth. Ple- ni
De- us, De- us Sa- ba- oth, Do- mi- nus De- us Sa- ba- oth. Ple- ni
De- us, De- us Sa- ba- oth, Do- mi- nus De- us Sa- ba- oth. Ple- ni
De- us Sa- ba- oth, Do- - mi- nus De- us Sa- ba- oth. Ple- ni

17
sunt cae- li, cae- li et ter- ra glo- - ri- a, glo- -
sunt cae- li, cae- li et ter- ra glo- ri- a, glo- - ri- a,
sunt cae- - li et ter- - ra glo- - ri- a tu- a,
sunt cae- li, cae- li et ter- ra glo- ri- a tu- a, glo-

23
- ri- a tu- a. Ho- san- na in ex- cel-
glo- ri- a tu- a.
glo- - ri- a tu- a. Ho- san- na in ex- cel- sis, ho- san- na in
- ri- a tu- a. Ho- san-
29
-sis, in ex- cel- sis, in ex-cel- sis, ho-san- na in ex- cel- sis, ho-
Ho- san- na in ex-cel- sis, in ex-cel- sis, ho-san- na in ex-cel- sis, in ex-cel-
ex- cel- sis, ho-san- na in ex-cel- sis, ho-san- na
-na in ex- cel- sis, in ex-cel- sis, ho- san- na in ex-cel- sis, ho-
35
-san- na in ex- cel- sis, ho-san-na in ex- cel- sis, in ex-cel- sis.
- sis, in ex-cel- - sis, ho- san- na in ex- cel- sis.
in ex- cel- - sis, ho- san- na in ex- cel- sis, in ex-cel- sis.
-san- na in ex- cel- sis, ho- san- na in ex- cel- - sis.

Agnus Dei

*See the editorial methods.

15
mi- se- re- re no- bis, mi- se-
do- na no- bis pa- cem, do- na
mi- - se- re- re, mi- se- re- re no-
do- - na no- bis, do- na no- bis pa-
- re no- - bis, mi- - se- re- re, mi-
- bis pa- - cem, do- - na no- bis, do-
mi- se- re- re no- bis, mi- se- re- re no-
do- na no- bis pa- cem, do- na no- bis pa-
20
-re- re no- bis, mi- se- re- re no- bis.
no- bis pa- cem, do- na no- bis pa- cem.
-bis, mi- se- re- - re no- bis.
-cem, do- na no- - bis pa- cem.
- se- re- re, mi- - se- re- re no- bis.
- na no- bis, do- - na no- bis pa- cem.
-bis, mi- - se- re- re, mi- se- re- re no- bis.
-cem, do- - na no- bis, do- na no- bis pa- cem.

Critical Report

Sources

The music of this edition has been taken from the manuscript Paris, Bibliothèque nationale de France, Département de la Musique, Rés. V^{ma} ms. 571, a bound volume of 239 folios containing some three hundred sacred Latin works in score. The manuscript was copied and assembled by organist and composer André Pechon from the 1630s through the 1680s, and while most of the works in the collection are preserved anonymously, over seventy can be attributed to Antoine Boesset. (Other composers attributed in the source include Carissimi, Bouzignac, Dumont, and Moulinié.) For more information about the precise dating of the manuscript contents and the attribution to Antoine Boesset, see " 'Boesset' Attributions in Rés. 571" and table 2 in the introduction to part 1.

Editorial Methods

This edition includes all works in Rés. 571 that can be attributed to Boesset, with the exception of those made up primarily of fauxbourdon and those that are small parts of lengthy chant works: "De profundis" (fol. 56v), "Lauda Jerusalem" (fols. 146v–147r), polyphonic settings of Hebrew letters for Tenebrae (fols. 183v–186v), Nunc dimittis (fols. 215r–v), and "Stabat mater" (fols. 215v–216r). As there is little systematic organization of Boesset's music within the source, this edition has reordered works so that they are organized first by genre, then in alphabetical order within genre, and finally in chronological order of copying. This system has been modified for parallel settings (i.e., mixed-voice and high-voice versions of the same piece), which appear in sequence. Folio numbers of the source are provided in the critical commentary. With the exception of the three masses, titles are editorial and are based on the textual incipit. The source includes the indications "à 4" and "à 5" for many of the works; these have been removed without comment.

Spelling, punctuation, and capitalization have been standardized and modernized in accordance with the *Liber Usualis* and the *Antiphonale Monasticum*. Source abbreviations and repetitions of text indicated only by an idem sign (⁒) or the first syllable or word of a phrase (e.g., "Al." = Alleluja) have been realized tacitly unless they are in some way questionable or ambiguous. Where voices are untexted, the underlay is usually so clear that text has been inserted tacitly. When the underlay is ambiguous—i.e., the text does not line up with the notes, there are more notes than syllables, or there are no slurs indicating how the text should be underlaid—a note has been made in the critical commentary. Source slurs used to indicate text underlay in untexted voices have been removed without comment. Ligatures in the source also indicate text underlay and are shown by full horizontal brackets. Word division follows modern rules for singing in Latin.

All voice names are editorial and appear in brackets, with two exceptions: the "Org." indications that appear in the late-copied section of the manuscript (expanded to "Orgue" without comment in the edition), and the designation "Plain chant," which appears in some chant sections of Rés. 571 and has been tacitly added to all chant versets for alternatim works. Voice names have been suggested in accordance with the clef of each part as follows:

Dessus = G2
Bas-dessus = C1
Haute-contre = C2
Haute-taille = C3
Taille = C4
Basse = F3 or F4
Basse continue and Orgue = F3 or F4

Treble clef has been substituted for C1 and C2 clefs, transposing treble clef for C3 and C4 clefs, and bass clef for F3 and F4 clefs. The range of each voice appears after the modern clef, key signature, and time signature. The bass voice and basse continue part share a staff in the source. The edition has separated these onto two staves and has tacitly altered the duration of notes in the bass voice at the ends of phrases to align with the upper parts. In some cases, the duration of notes at the ends of phrases in other voices has been altered to be consistent with the surrounding parts and has been reported in the critical commentary.

Repetition schemes in the source have been tacitly modernized and clarified. The source typically indicates first and second endings by showing the first few notes and/or text of the repeated passage following the end of the piece; in many cases, either the term "segno" or a 𝄋 also serve to guide the performer. These indications have been converted to modern first and second endings without comment. Source directives such as "Sanctus ut supra" have been replaced with modern da capo or dal segno indications without brackets. When necessary, repeated sections have been written out and reported in the critical commentary.

As was common practice in French liturgical music of this time, the source includes only a single polyphonic verse for each of the Agnus Dei movements (ending in "miserere nobis") in the three complete masses. Since the entire three-part text was presumably meant to be performed, and since it is a fairly simple matter to substitute "dona nobis pacem" for "miserere nobis" in the third and final line of the text, this edition has provided the "dona nobis pacem" text as an editorial addition. In the *Messe à 5 du 3e transposé* and *Messe à 4 du 11e mode,* a repeat sign has been added, and a second line of underlay has been provided when the text changes for the final verse. For the alternatim *Messe de Boesset du Tiers,* the editorial addition has been written out in full, with the initial polyphonic Agnus Dei returning after the chant statement but appearing with the altered final line of text.

Chant portions of the alternatim canticles have been taken from Rés. 571 and the *Antiphonier ... de Montmartre.* The tones for Magnificats (1), (2), and (5) appear in Rés. 571 on fol. 219r (see plate 4), one of two pages of chant that also include versets for the alternatim hymns published in part 1 of this edition. The tones for these Magnificats are concordant with the *Antiphonier ... de Montmartre* (see plate 3), though the note values of Magnificats (2) and (5) are halved in Rés. 571. As Rés. 571 only provides text underlay for the first two verses of the Magnificat, the rhythm of the remaining verses is taken from another, through-composed, Magnificat chant in the *Antiphonier ... de Montmartre.* Alternatim versets for Te Deum (2) are also taken from the *Antiphonier ... de Montmartre.* Since all the chants in Rés. 571 appear in white notation, transcriptions based on the black notation of the *Antiphonier ... de Montmartre* have been changed to white for consistency. Following the convention of the *Antiphonier ... de Montmartre* (in which the chant is written an octave lower that it would sound), melodies have been transposed up an octave.

Chant versets for the alternatim *Messe de Boesset du Tiers* have been taken from Rés. 571 and transcribed as they appear in the source, with white breves and semibreves. Chant intonations for the Gloria and Credo movements of all three masses have been taken from the *Missale Romanum* (Paris, 1626). The breves and semibreves of the *Missale Romanum* have been retained and converted to white notation for the *Messe de Boesset du Tiers* to be consistent with the alternatim versets in Rés. 571. By contrast, intonation rhythms for the *Messe à 5 du 3e transposé* and *Messe à 4 du 11e mode* have been transcribed according to the "equal note" principle recommended in Pierre-Benoît de Jumilhac's *Science et pratique du plain-chant* (1673). For more information about the appropriate performance of chant rhythms, see "Notes on Performance" in the introduction to part 1.

The edition reflects the original barring of the source. The appearance of barlines in the source differs according to copying period, and the method of transcribing double barlines varies throughout the edition. In works copied during the early and middle periods of the manuscript (fols. 1v–177v; see table 2 in the introduction to part 1), the paper is pre-ruled from top to bottom with barlines (see plates 1 and 2); in some places, Pechon drew an additional barline by hand to indicate the end of a section—though the additional barline did not always appear in all parts. Regardless of whether this hand-drawn barline appeared in all or in only some voices, these barlines have been transcribed as double barlines in the edition. For the late-copied group of works, the paper was ruled as the copying proceeded, but, again, Pechon drew an additional barline by hand at major structural divisions. These places have also been rendered as double barlines in the edition. Exceptions to this policy are reported in the critical commentary. Occasionally Pechon placed the equivalent of two measures between pre-ruled barlines, especially when approaching the end of a line. In these cases, missing barlines have been tacitly added. Predrawn barlines in passages of unmetered fauxbourdon in Te Deum (2) have been tacitly removed.

The time signatures of the source—**C**, **¢**, **2**, and **3**—have been retained wherever possible; **¢** therefore appears with both two half notes and four half notes per measure. Proportional time signatures, such as **¢3**, have been converted to their modern equivalent, and the original time signature appears above the staff. For shifts between duple and triple meter in which the tactus (rather than the beat) remains constant, an equivalency has been provided above the staff. Superfluous meters, such as the reiteration of a meter at the beginning of a section, have been tacitly removed. Editorial meters appear in brackets.

The original note values are used; that is, transcription is at the ratio 1:1. Notes that continue past a barline in the source have been divided into appropriate values and connected with a tie. Final notes of sections or whole works have been regularized to a whole note or breve with a fermata, unless a moving voice requires the note to be longer than notated in the source. Fermatas do not always appear consistently in all parts; when they appear in only one part, they have been tacitly realized in the remaining parts. All other editorial fermatas appear in brackets. Source beaming, which often indicates text underlay, has been changed to conform to modern beaming practices.

Source accidentals are typically valid only for the note itself and any immediate or very close repetition; in the edition, accidentals follow the modern practice by which they are valid for the entire measure in which they occur, including the unmetered fauxbourdon passages in Te Deum (2). Editorial accidentals are enclosed in square brackets; added cautionary accidentals appear in parentheses. Accidentals made superfluous by modern barring and convention have been eliminated without comment.

Critical Commentary

Critical notes list rejected or ambiguous readings from the source and alternative readings taken from the *Antiphonier ... de Montmartre.* Notes are located in the score by measure number and part name. When specific notes and rests in a measure are cited, tied noteheads are numbered individually, and rests are counted separately from notes. The following abbreviations are used in the paragraphs below: M(m). = measure(s), D1–3 = Dessus 1–3, BD = Bas-dessus, HC = Haute-contre, HT = Haute-taille, T = Taille, B = Basse, B.c. = Basse continue, Org. = Orgue. The pitch system used throughout is that in which c′ represents middle C.

1. *Magnificat (1)*

Sources. Polyphonic setting, fols. 155v–156v. Magnificat tone, fol. 219r. The Magnificat tone also appears in halved note values on fol. 155v (see plate 2); both are melodically concordant with the *Antiphonier . . . de Montmartre,* 520. The Magnificat tone on fol. 155v also includes a meter of ¢ and appears to include barlines, but these "barlines" were pre-ruled on the page, and the Magnificat tone does not fit within ¢. Rhythm of subsequent verses based on *Antiphonier . . . de Montmartre,* 523–25.

Notes. M. 3 has two sketches for B and B.c., both of which are unsatisfactory: one is crossed out; the second has a total of five beats; beats 4–5 are e dotted quarter, d 8th (see plate 2). M. 15, B and B.c., note 2 is A. M. 24, HC, note is f′. M. 31, D2, half note followed by half rest. M. 60, D3, whole note. Mm. 79–81, D3, notes are g′–a′–b′–c″–b′–c″–d″.

2. *Magnificat (2)*

Sources. Polyphonic setting, fols. 157r–158r. Magnificat tone, fol. 219r. Rhythm of subsequent verses based on *Antiphonier . . . de Montmartre*, 523–25.

Notes. M. 7, D1, rhythm is dotted 8th, 16th, quarter, dotted quarter, 8th. M. 25, D2, note is e′. M. 26, B.c., note 4 is d. M. 28, D3, whole note. M. 39, D3, note 1 is e″. M. 60, D2, beat 2 is quarter note; divided into two 8th notes to fit underlay. M. 86, B and B.c., note 1 missing.

3. *Magnificat (3)*

Source. Fols. 29r–30v.

Comment. Marked "a 4 v SSDB et org. de Boesset" in Brossard's hand and "Boesset" in Pechon's hand.

Notes. M. 18, D2, note 3 is e″. M. 27, B and B.c., note 1 is g. M. 32, D2, note 3, "-ti-" moved from m. 31, note 4. M. 32, D2 and HC, underlay unclear. Mm. 69–72, HC, underlay unclear; edition based on clearer underlay in B. Mm. 110–11, B.c., tie missing.

4. *Magnificat (4)*

Source. Fols. 191v–192v.

Notes. M. 7, D2, note 3 is d″. M. 38, D1 and BD, half note followed by half rest. M. 64, Org., note 1 is c. M. 97, BD, note 1 is g′. M. 103, fermata and double barline in all parts.

5. *Magnificat (5)*

Sources. Polyphonic setting, fols. 192v–193v. Magnificat tone, fol. 219r. Rhythm of subsequent verses based on *Antiphonier . . . de Montmartre,* 523–25.

6. *Magnificat (6)*

Source. Fols. 221v–223r.

Notes. Mm. 6, 13, 26, 35, 51, 59, 72, 82, 96, 105, fermata and double barline in all parts; as it is unusual for a through-composed Magnificat to pause at the end of each line, these barlines and fermatas are likely a scribal error. M. 18, D1, underlay unclear. M. 21, Org., note 3 is a. M. 82, HC, note is a′.

7. *Te Deum (1)*

Source. Fols. 178r–180r.

Comment. HC and HT reversed in source.

Notes. M. 40, HC, whole note. M. 78, D, note 4 is d″. M. 92, D, underlay unclear. Mm. 124–27, text is "famulis tuis" rather than "tuis famulis." M. 144, HT, note 2 is c′. M. 145, HT, notes 1–3 are d′ 8th, d′ 8th slurred to e′ quarter.

8. *Te Deum (2)*

Sources. Polyphonic setting, fols. 180r–181v. Chant versets, *Antiphonier . . . de Montmartre,* 512–17.

Notes. M. 37, B and Org., note 3 missing (incomplete measure). M. 96, BD, note 2 has ♯. Mm. 111–16, B, source has only a single statement of "venturus"; underlay as follows: m. 113, note 1 through m. 115, note 3, "-tu-"; m. 116, "-rus."

9. *Beatus vir*

Source. Fols. 190r–191v.

Note. M. 127, BD, notes 2–3 are b′–c″.

10. *Dixit Dominus*

Source. Fols. 158r–160r.

Notes. Mm. 8, 16, 31, fermata and double barline. Mm. 73–77, D2 and BD reversed. M. 81, D2, half note followed by half rest. Mm. 88–96, D1 and D2 reversed. M. 96, double barline.

11. *Ecce quam bonum*

Source. Fols. 182v–183r.

Comment. Source indicates responsorial structure by writing out first measure of "Ecce quam" and 𝄋; repetition of response written out in full in edition.

Note. M. 76, HC, "-rum" is on note 1.

12. *Laetatus sum*

Source. Fols. 161v–162v.

Note. Mm. 1–9, B, source implies that text should be underlaid.

13. Laudate pueri (1)

Source. Fols. 160r–161r.

Note. M. 53, D2, note 2–m. 54, note 1, tie missing.

14. Laudate pueri (2)

Source. Fols. 219v–221r.

Comment. HC and HT reversed.

Notes. M. 27, Org., note 2 has figures 4–3. M. 57, HT, notes 2–3 are e′–f′. M. 75, HT, note 1 is half note. M. 79, D1, HT, Org., whole note.

15. Kyrie

Source. Fol. 169v.

Notes. Mm. 22–26, BD, source underlay as follows: m. 22, note 2, "e-"; m. 23, note 1, "-lei-"; m. 24, note 4, "-son"; m. 24, note 5, "e-"; m. 25, note 1, "-le-"; m. 26, note 2, "-i-"; m. 26, note 3, "-son." Mm. 25–26, D1, underlay is "e-lei-son," with the second syllable falling on m. 26, note 2.

16. Sanctus, Benedictus

Source. Fols. 169v–170r.

17. Agnus Dei

Source. Polyphonic setting and chant, fol. 170v.

Comment. Repetition of polyphonic "Agnus Dei" written out in edition.

18. Libera me

Source. Fols. 154v–155v.

Notes. M. 11, B and B.c., final note is F. M. 34, all parts, whole note. M. 52, D1, notes 1–2, text is "illa." Mm. 55–56, D2, underlay unclear. Mm. 79–80, D1, "requiem" in source. Mm. 82–83, HC, underlay unclear. M. 87, HC, underlay unclear.

19. Pie Jesu

Source. Fol. 177v.

Messe à 5 du 3e transposé

Sources. Fols. 134r–139v. Gloria and Credo intonations taken from *Missale Romanum,* 243–44, and transposed up a fourth.

Comments. Marked "Messe a 5 du 3e transpose" in Pechon's hand. Pechon is using Zarlino's later twelve-mode system, this being equivalent to medieval mode 1 (transposed).

Gloria

Notes. Mm. 67–68, D1, tie missing. M. 71, D2, note 2, "-re" moved from m. 72, note 3.

Credo

Notes. M. 1, B.c., note 3 has ♯. M. 3, B.c., note 1 appears at end of m. 2, leaving five beats in m. 2 and three beats in m. 3. Mm. 32–34, D2, entry is measure early but corrected by one-measure gap. M. 65, B.c., note 4 is e♮. M. 70, D1, note 2 is g′. Mm. 125–30, D1, entry is half measure early.

Sanctus

Notes. M. 52, D2, half note followed by half rest. M. 56, D3, whole note.

Agnus Dei

Note. M. 5, B and B.c., note is half note; subsequent notes are half measure early until corrected by gap in m. 9.

Messe de Boesset du Tiers

Sources. Fols. 170v–174r. The alternatim chants are provided in the source. Gloria and Credo intonations taken from *Missale Romanum,* 243–44, and converted to white notation.

Comments. Beginning of work marked "Messe de Boesset du Tiers" in unidentified hand. Marked "Boesset" at end of Agnus Dei in Pechon's hand.

Kyrie

Comments. The source provides two polyphonic Kyrie statements (mm. 1–8 and 10–16), a single statement of the Christe chant, and the polyphonic Christe section. The Kyrie chant is missing from the source; the chant appearing in measure 9 is an editorial realization based on the Christe chant. The alternation of chant with polyphony and the return of the complete Kyrie (mm. 28–43) are editorial recommendations and reflect the performance practice of French liturgical music during Boesset's time.

Note. M. 26, all parts, whole note.

Gloria

Notes. Mm. 49–50, barline missing; source has single measure ending with whole note in all parts. M. 53, D2, whole note followed by half rest.

Credo

Notes. M. 34, B and B.c., notes 1–3 are f–d–c. M. 57, D1, missing from source; measure is an editorial reconstruction. M. 72, source omitted "regni"; measure is an editorial reconstruction.

Agnus Dei

Note. M. 17, chant notated in blackened semibreves and marked "le chant entrelassé."

Messe à 4 du 11e mode

Sources. Fols. 50r–54r. Gloria and Credo intonations taken from *Missale Romanum,* 243–44, and transposed up a fifth.

Comments. Marked "Messe a 4 du iie mode" in Pechon's hand and "de Boësset" in Brossard's at beginning of Kyrie; marked "Boesset" at end of Agnus Dei in Pechon's hand.

Kyrie

Notes. M. 6–10, HC, underlay unclear. M. 21, B and B.c., note 1 is A.

Gloria

Note. M. 88, B and B.c., note 4 is c.

Credo

Notes. M. 61, HC, underlay unclear; note 3 is d′. M. 126, D2, note 3 has augmentation dot.

Sanctus

Notes. M. 5, no barline. M. 8, no barline. M. 24, no barline.